# EXPANDING TACTICS FOR LISTENING

## Second Edition

Jack C. Richards

OXFORD

UNIVERSITY PRESS

# OXFORD
UNIVERSITY PRESS

198 Madison Avenue
New York, NY 10016 USA

Great Clarendon Street, Oxford OX2 6DP UK

Oxford University Press is a department of the University of Oxford.
It furthers the University's objective of excellence in research, scholarship,
and education by publishing worldwide in

Oxford  New York

Auckland  Cape Town  Dar es Salaam  Hong Kong  Karachi
Kuala Lumpur  Madrid  Melbourne  Mexico City  Nairobi
New Delhi  Shanghai  Taipei  Toronto

With offices in

Argentina  Austria  Brazil  Chile  Czech Republic  France  Greece
Guatemala  Hungary  Italy  Japan  Poland  Portugal  Singapore
South Korea  Switzerland  Thailand  Turkey  Ukraine  Vietnam

OXFORD and OXFORD ENGLISH are registered trademarks of
Oxford University Press

© Oxford University Press 2004

Database right Oxford University Press (maker)

Editorial Manager: Nancy Leonhardt
Managing Editor: Jeff Krum
Editor: Joseph McGasko
Associate Editor: Mike Boyle
Art Director: Lynn Luchetti
Design Project Manager: Maj-Britt Hagsted
Designer: Michael Steinhofer
Art Editors: Justine Eun, Andrea Suffredini
Production Manager: Shanta Persaud
Production Controller: Eve Wong

ISBN : 978 0 19 438459 9 (Student Book with CD Pack)
ISBN : 978 0 19 438844 3 (Student Book without CD)

Printed in China

10 9 8 7 6 5

ACKNOWLEDGMENTS

*Cover design by* Lee Anne Dollison
*Cover photography by* Arnold Katz Photography; PhotoDisc; MPTA
Stock/Masterfile; Barbara Haynor/Index Stock Location and studio
photography: Arnold Katz Photography

*Illustrations and Realia by* Doug Archer, Barbara Bastian, Ron Bell,
Carlos Castellanos, John Courtney, Mike D'Antuono/Studio Design,
Douglas Day, Jim Delapine, Stan Gorernan, Jon Keegan,
Scott MacNeill/MacNeill & Macintosh, Jeff Seaver, Paul Weiner,
www.illustrationweb.com/Mark Watkinson

*The publishers would like to thank the following for their permission to reproduce
photographs:*
AFP/CORBIS; Forrest Anderson/TimePix; Shaun Best/Reuters;
Bettmann/CORBIS; BrandXPictures; Craig J. Brown/IndexStock; Camelot/Pacific
Press Service; Jason Cohn/ZUMA/TimePix; Comstock; CORBIS SYGMA;
Thomas Craig/IndexStock; David Cumming, Michael Dalder/Reuters;
Kjeld Duits/Japanese Streets; Eye Ubiquitous/CORBIS; Eyebyte/Alamy;
Warren Flager/Indexstock; FoodPix; Wallace Garrison/IndexStock;
Getty/PhotoDisc; Mark Gibson/IndexStock; Peter Griffith/Masterfile;
Chip Henderson/IndexStock; Hulton-Deutsch Collection/CORBIS;
Mark Hunt/IndexStock; Richard Hutchings/CORBIS; ImageState; IT STOCK
INT'L/IndexStock; David Jacobs/IndexStock; Andre Jenny/Alamy;
Li Jiangang/ImagineChina; John Henley Photography/CORBIS; Kelly-Mooney
Photography/CORBIS; The Kobal Collection; Mark Lewis/Alamy; Andrew Liu;
John Lund/CORBIS; Robert Maass/CORBIS; Lawrence Manning/CORBIS;
Perry Mastrovito/CORBIS; The New England School of English, Cambridge MA;
Steve Ogilvy; Vic Pigula/Alamy; Michael Pole/CORBIS; Steve Prezant/CORBIS;
Retna Ltd.; Reuters NewMedia Inc./CORBIS; Rick Gayle Studio, Inc./CORBIS;
Royal Geographical Society/Alamy; Royalty-Free/CORBIS; The Sharper Image;
Stephen Saks/IndexStock; Ariel Skelley/CORBIS; StockImage/ImageState;
STR/Reuters; Scott Suchman/ImagesState; SuperStock/PictureQuest; TimePix;
Time Life Pictures; David Turnley/CORBIS; Pierre Vauthey/CORBIS; Diana
Walker/TimePix; Roger Werth/Woodfin Camp/TimePix; M. Winkel/Masterfile;
Caroline Woodham/ImageState; Sat Yip/SuperStock; Zach Holmes
Photography/Zach Holmes

# Contents

# Scope and Sequence

| Unit | Themes | Skills |
|------|--------|--------|
| 1 | Greetings<br>Small talk | Listening for greetings and introductions<br>Listening for topics<br>Listening for attitudes<br>Listening and making inferences<br>Listening and making predictions |
| 2 | Jobs<br>Job interviews | Listening for gist<br>Listening for jobs<br>Listening for details |
| 3 | Business | Listening for negative information<br>Listening for gist<br>Listening for details |
| 4 | Gadgets<br>Machines | Listening for gist<br>Listening for details |
| 5 | People<br>Character traits | Listening for gist<br>Listening for praise or criticism<br>Listening for details |
| 6 | Food<br>Recipes | Listening for gist<br>Listening for details |
| 7 | Housing | Listening for gist<br>Listening for negative information<br>Listening for details |
| 8 | Complaints<br>Neighborhoods<br>Apartments | Listening for gist<br>Listening for details<br>Listening for agreement and disagreement |
| 9 | Friends<br>Dating<br>Invitations | Listening for gist<br>Listening for details |
| 10 | Television | Listening for topics<br>Listening for gist<br>Listening for details<br>Listening for agreement and disagreement<br>Listening for attitudes |
| 11 | Cities<br>Travel | Listening for details<br>Listening for gist |
| 12 | Cities<br>Improvements | Listening for topics<br>Listening for gist<br>Listening for details<br>Listening for suggestions |

| Unit | Themes | Skills |
|------|--------|--------|
| 13 | Holidays<br>Celebrations | Listening for gist<br>Listening for details<br>Listening for likes and dislikes |
| 14 | Fashion<br>Clothes | Listening for gist<br>Listening for time references<br>Listening for details |
| 15 | Preferences | Listening for preferences<br>Listening for topics<br>Listening for agreement and disagreement<br>Listening for details |
| 16 | Messages | Listening for gist<br>Listening for attitudes<br>Listening for details |
| 17 | Past events | Listening for gist<br>Listening for sequence<br>Listening for attitudes<br>Listening and making predictions<br>Listening for details |
| 18 | Vacations | Listening for preferences<br>Listening for details<br>Listening for gist |
| 19 | News reports | Listening for topics<br>Listening for gist<br>Listening for details |
| 20 | Opinions | Listening for topics<br>Listening for gist<br>Listening for opinions<br>Listening for reasons<br>Listening for details |
| 21 | Famous people | Listening for gist<br>Listening for details<br>Listening for sequence |
| 22 | Food<br>Nutrition | Listening for gist<br>Listening for suggestions<br>Listening for details<br>Listening for sequence |
| 23 | Predicaments | Listening for gist<br>Listening for details<br>Listening for attitudes |
| 24 | Issues<br>Problems | Listening for gist<br>Listening for comparisons<br>Listening for topics<br>Listening for details |

# Introduction

## Tactics for Listening

*Tactics for Listening* is a three-level series of listening textbooks for students of English as a second or foreign language. Taken together, the three levels make up a comprehensive course in listening skills in American English.

## Expanding Tactics for Listening

*Expanding Tactics for Listening* is the third level of the *Tactics for Listening* series. It is intended for intermediate students who have studied English previously but need further practice in understanding everyday conversational language. It contains 24 units. It can be used as the main text for a listening course, as a complementary text in a conversation course, or as the basis for a language laboratory course. Each unit features a topic that relates to the everyday life and experience of adults and young adults. The topics have been chosen for their frequency in conversation and their interest to learners. A wide variety of stimulating and useful activities are included to give students graded practice in listening.

## Student Book

In the *Expanding Tactics for Listening* Student Book, students practice listening for a variety of purposes and hear examples of different types of spoken English including casual conversations, instructions, directions, requests, descriptions, apologies, and suggestions. Essential listening skills are practiced throughout the text. These skills include listening for key words, details, and gist; listening and making inferences; listening for attitudes; listening to questions and responding; and recognizing and identifying information.

Each unit has five sections. The first section, "Getting Ready," introduces the topic of the unit and presents key vocabulary for the unit listening tasks. The next three sections, each entitled "Let's Listen," are linked to conversations or monologues recorded on cassette or CD. These sections provide task-based, graded listening practice. Finally, there is a follow-up speaking activity, "Over to You," which relates to the theme and listening tasks of the unit.

## Audio Program

The complete audio program for *Expanding Tactics for Listening* Student Book is available as a set of three Class CDs or Cassettes. In addition, the Student Book with CD contains a Student CD on the inside back cover for home study. The CD includes the listening passages for the final Let's Listen section of each unit.

## Teacher's Book

The *Expanding Tactics for Listening* Teacher's Book provides extensive lesson plans for each unit, answer keys, optional activities, vocabulary lists, and a photocopiable tapescript of the recorded material. The Teacher's Book also includes photocopiable midterm and final tests, as well as worksheets (one per unit) that offer additional speaking activities. The audio program for the midterm and final tests is included on a CD on the inside back cover.

## Test Booklet

The *Expanding Tactics for Listening* Test Booklet contains photocopiable tests for each unit of the Student Book. The audio program for the unit tests is included on a CD on the inside back cover.

# UNIT 1 Small Talk

## 1. Getting Ready

Are these expressions used to greet someone you know or to introduce yourself to someone you don't know? Check (✓) the correct answer.

|  | Greet | Introduce |
|---|:---:|:---:|
| 1. I don't think we've met. | ☐ | ☑ |
| 2. Hi! I haven't seen you for a long time! | ☐ | ☐ |
| 3. Hello. My name's Kate. | ☐ | ☐ |
| 4. Hi. I'm Don. I just started working here. | ☐ | ☐ |
| 5. Hi, nice to see you again. | ☐ | ☐ |
| 6. Betsy! How are you doing? | ☐ | ☐ |
| 7. Hey, aren't you in my class? I'm Tom Crane. | ☐ | ☐ |

## 2. Let's Listen

People are talking at a party. Have they met before? Listen and check (✓) the correct answer.

| | Have met before | Haven't met before |
|---|:---:|:---:|
| 1. | ☐ | ☑ |
| 2. | ☐ | ☐ |
| 3. | ☐ | ☐ |
| 4. | ☐ | ☐ |
| 5. | ☐ | ☐ |
| 6. | ☐ | ☐ |

# 3. Let's Listen

People are making small talk. What are they talking about? Listen and circle the correct answer.

1. **a.** clothes     3. **a.** the weather     5. **a.** school
   **b.** school               **b.** a vacation        **b.** work
   **c.** work                 **c.** health problems   **c.** apartments

2. **a.** work       4. **a.** school            6. **a.** work
   **b.** school               **b.** work              **b.** family
   **c.** friends             **c.** a new boyfriend   **c.** school

Task 2

Listen again. Does the last person speaking want to continue or end the conversation? Check (✓) the correct answer.

|  | Continue the conversation | End the conversation |
|---|---|---|
| 1. | ☐ | ☑ |
| 2. | ☐ | ☐ |
| 3. | ☐ | ☐ |
| 4. | ☐ | ☐ |
| 5. | ☐ | ☐ |
| 6. | ☐ | ☐ |

# 4. Let's Listen

**Task 1**

**People are making small talk. What question are they answering?
Circle the correct answer.**

1. a. Are you here on vacation?
   b. Do you like living here? *(circled)*

2. a. Do you think English is difficult?
   b. Why are you studying English?

3. a. How old are your children?
   b. How many children do you have?

4. a. What kind of work do you do?
   b. What kind of job would you like?

5. a. When did you arrive?
   b. Have you been having fun here?

6. a. Where did you go on vacation?
   b. Where are you from?

**Task 2**

**Listen again. Circle the best response.**

1. a. I'm glad you like it here. *(circled)*
   b. That's too bad.
   c. Me, neither.

2. a. I like those videos, too.
   b. Why don't you like them?
   c. I agree. They're terrible.

3. a. Thanks, anyway.
   b. I agree. Two is enough.
   c. I'm glad you and your husband agree.

4. a. Thanks. I'd love to.
   b. Sorry. I'm busy that day.
   c. I'd love to see your house.

5. a. You'll love the beach.
   b. What kind of car will you buy?
   c. Good idea. The scenery is great there.

6. a. Yeah, I think I will.
   b. Really? Why not?
   c. You're right. I shouldn't go there.

# Over to You: What do you study?

**Task 1**

**Work in pairs. Think of two questions to ask about each small-talk topic.
Write them under each picture.**

School

1. *What do you study?*

2. _____

Work

1. _____

2. _____

The weather

1. _____

2. _____

Hobbies

1. _____

2. _____

**Task 2**

**Move around the classroom and make small talk with your classmates.
Use the questions from Task 1.**

**Example:** **A:** What do you study?

**B:** I study engineering. And you?

**A:** I study…

## 1. Getting Ready

Have you ever had these part-time jobs? Would you like to have them?
Check (✓) your answers and compare them with a partner.

| | Part-time jobs I've had | Part-time jobs I'd like to have |
|---|---|---|
| convenience store clerk | ☐ | ☐ |
| lifeguard | ☐ | ☐ |
| coffee shop employee | ☐ | ☐ |
| camp counselor | ☐ | ☐ |
| pizza delivery person | ☐ | ☐ |
| fast food cook | ☐ | ☐ |
| other: _____ | ☐ | ☐ |

## 2. Let's Listen 💿

Students are interviewing for part-time jobs. Have they ever done the work before?
Listen and check (✓) the correct answer.

| | Has done it before | Has done something similar | Has never done it before |
|---|---|---|---|
| 1. | ☐ | ☐ | ☑ |
| 2. | ☐ | ☐ | ☐ |
| 3. | ☐ | ☐ | ☐ |
| 4. | ☐ | ☐ | ☐ |
| 5. | ☐ | ☐ | ☐ |
| 6. | ☐ | ☐ | ☐ |

# 3. Let's Listen 💿

**People are talking about their part-time jobs. What jobs do they have?**
**Listen and number the pictures.**

A.

B.

C.

D.

E. *1*

F.

**Task 2**

**Listen again. What does each person dislike about his or her job?**
**Circle the correct answer.**

1. **a.** the desserts
   **b.** the heat
   **c.** the money

2. **a.** the uniform
   **b.** the kids
   **c.** the money

3. **a.** the hours
   **b.** the movies
   **c.** the soda and popcorn

4. **a.** the boring work
   **b.** the money
   **c.** the location

5. **a.** the work
   **b.** the location
   **c.** the money

6. **a.** the people
   **b.** the money
   **c.** the hours

# 4. Let's Listen

## Task 1

People are talking about their part-time jobs. What do they like best about their jobs? Circle the correct answer.

1. **a.** She works outdoors.
   **b.** She meets interesting people.
   **c.** She travels to South America.

2. **a.** The salary is good.
   **b.** He has flexible hours.
   **c.** He has nice co-workers.

3. **a.** It's relaxing work.
   **b.** He is well paid.
   **c.** He enjoys working with children.

4. **a.** The hours are long.
   **b.** Her co-workers are terrific.
   **c.** She is well paid.

5. **a.** She likes working outside.
   **b.** It's really stressful.
   **c.** She's met some famous people.

6. **a.** He is very well paid.
   **b.** The hours are good.
   **c.** The work is easy.

## Task 2

Listen again. What important skills or knowledge do the people need for their jobs? Write the correct letter.

1. It's really important to ___
2. The most important thing is to ___
3. It's important to ___
4. It's important to ___
5. It's important to ___
6. The most important thing is to ___

a. know what you're teaching.
b. have a friendly voice.
c. know a second language.
d. have experience with computers.
e. know what you sell.
f. have good listening skills.

# Over to You: Have you ever been a...?

Task 1

What are some popular part-time jobs? Write five more jobs.

1. _____lifeguard_____
2. _____
3. _____
4. _____
5. _____
6. _____

Task 2

Work in pairs. Student A is an employer. Student B is a student interviewing for a part-time job. Practice the conversation below.

**A:** Have you ever been a (1) lifeguard before?

**B:** No, I haven't, but I have a lot of experience (2) working with children.

**A:** (3) Interesting. Can you (4) swim?

**B:** (5) Yes. I'm an excellent swimmer.

Task 3

Work in pairs. Have two more conversations like the one in Task 2. Use this information.

| | |
|---|---|
| (1) waiter | fast food cook |
| (2) working in restaurants | cooking at home |
| (3) Great. | I see. |
| (4) work on weekends | cook many orders at once |
| (5) Actually, I'd rather not. | I don't know. But I can try. |

Task 4

Work in pairs. Take turns role-playing the situation in Task 2. Use your own information.

# UNIT 3 Successful Businesses

## 1. Getting Ready

What do you think makes a business successful? Number the items in each list from 1 (most important) to 5 (least important). Compare your answers with a partner.

| A restaurant |
|---|
| ___ location |
| ___ prices |
| ___ service |
| ___ atmosphere |
| ___ other: _____ |

| A language school |
|---|
| ___ location |
| ___ staff |
| ___ courses |
| ___ popularity |
| ___ other: _____ |

| A hotel |
|---|
| ___ price |
| ___ rooms |
| ___ location |
| ___ facilities |
| ___ other: _____ |

## 2. Let's Listen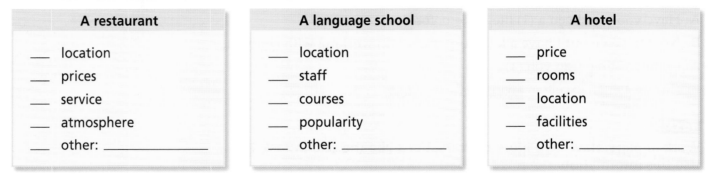

People are talking about different businesses. What do they dislike about each place? Listen and circle the correct answer.

1. **a.** food
   **b.** service

2. **a.** location
   **b.** prices

3. **a.** popularity
   **b.** prices

4. **a.** service
   **b.** location

5. **a.** prices
   **b.** service

6. **a.** clothes
   **b.** service

# 3. Let's Listen

**Task 1**

People are talking about different businesses. Listen and number the pictures.

A.

B.

C.

D.

E.

F.

**Task 2**

Listen again. What do the people like about each business?
Circle the correct answer.

1. **a.** location
   **b.** service
   **c.** music

2. **a.** prices
   **b.** facilities
   **c.** teachers

3. **a.** staff
   **b.** speed
   **c.** prices

4. **a.** atmosphere
   **b.** staff
   **c.** prices

5. **a.** location
   **b.** prices
   **c.** size

6. **a.** prices
   **b.** quality
   **c.** displays

# 4. Let's Listen

## Task 1

People are talking about businesses they own. What does each person think is most important? Listen and circle the correct answer.

1.

Tommy Miura, Ichigo Restaurant

   **a.** the fish
   **b.** chefs
   **c.** service

2.

Sally White, Odyssey Travel

   **a.** the website
   **b.** a good value
   **c.** speed

3.

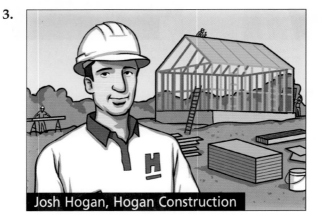

Josh Hogan, Hogan Construction

   **a.** speed
   **b.** prices
   **c.** quality

4.

Wendy Martinez, Fashion City

   **a.** displays
   **b.** quality
   **c.** prices

## Task 2

Listen again. What other important things do the people mention?
Write the correct letter.

1. ___      **a.** convenience

2. ___      **b.** food

3. ___      **c.** prices

4. ___      **d.** quality

# **Over to You:** Your own restaurant

Task 1

**Work in groups. Your group is going to open a new restaurant.
Discuss these questions.**

1. What kind of restaurant will you open?
2. Where will it be?
3. What will it look like?
4. What kind of food will you serve?
5. How many customers will it seat?
6. How many employees will work there?
7. What special features will it have to attract customers?

Task 2

**Work in groups. Draw a picture of your restaurant, the restaurant sign,
or the menu.**

Task 3

**Work in pairs. Compare pictures with a partner. Have your partner guess
what kind of restaurant your group will open.**

Example:   **A:** What do you think of my menu?

          **B:** Wow, that looks nice.

          **A:** What kind of restaurant do you think it is?

          **B:** It looks like a Mexican restaurant.

# UNIT 4 Gadgets and Machines

## 1. Getting Ready

What do you think these gadgets are? What do you think they are used for?
Compare your answers with a partner.

**Example:** Gadget A could be a microphone.

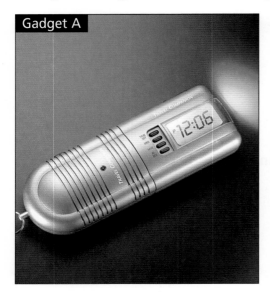

Gadget A

Gadget B

**Useful expressions**

This is probably a...
This could be a...
This is used for...

## 2. Let's Listen 💿

People are talking about these gadgets. Listen and number the pictures.

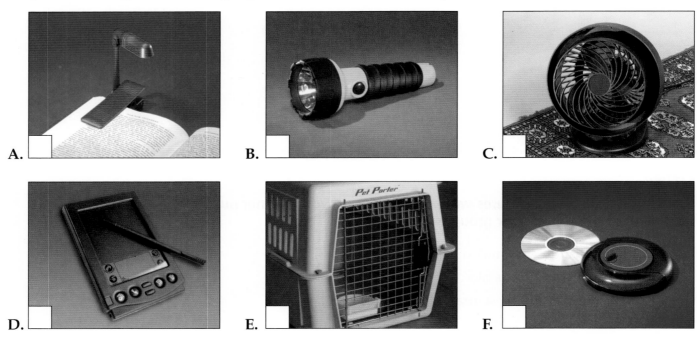

A.

B.

C.

D.

E.

F.

# 3. Let's Listen 🔊

**People are having problems using these machines. Listen and number the pictures.**

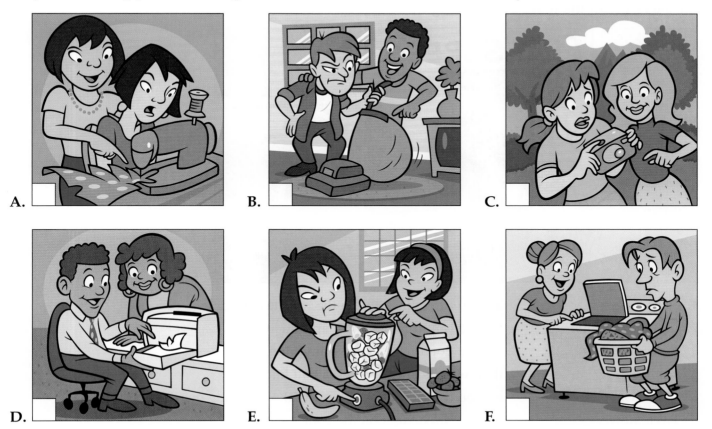

A.

B.

C.

D.

E.

F.

Task 2

**Listen again. What is the problem with each machine? Circle the correct answer.**

1. a. She needs more film.
   b. The batteries are dead.
   c. It's too dirty.

2. a. He put in too much soap.
   b. He put in too much clothing.
   c. He put in too much money.

3. a. There's no dust bag.
   b. The dust bag is empty.
   c. The dust bag is full.

4. a. She used the wrong paper size.
   b. She put in too much paper.
   c. She didn't use enough paper.

5. a. The dress is the wrong color.
   b. The needle is too big.
   c. The needle is too small.

6. a. She put in too much sugar.
   b. She put in too much fruit.
   c. She put in too much ice.

# 4. Let's Listen

People are talking about machines and appliances. Listen and match the products on the left with the features on the right.

1. flat screen TV _f_
2. laptop computer ___
3. air conditioner ___
4. clothes dryer ___
5. dishwasher ___
6. lawn mower ___

a. You can adjust it with the remote control.
b. You can fit it in a small apartment.
c. You don't have to rinse anything.
d. It weighs only one and a half kilos.
e. You can run it for an hour without adding gas.
f. You can hang it on the wall.

Task 2

Listen again. Are these statements true or false? Check (✓) the correct answer.

|  | True | False |
|---|:---:|:---:|
| 1. You shouldn't put it near a window. | ☐ | ☐ |
| 2. You should keep it in the case when you carry it. | ☐ | ☐ |
| 3. You should open the windows when you use it. | ☐ | ☐ |
| 4. You shouldn't touch the lint filter. | ☐ | ☐ |
| 5. You shouldn't put any soap in it. | ☐ | ☐ |
| 6. You shouldn't put your hand under the machine. | ☐ | ☐ |

# Over to You: What's your favorite gadget?

Task 1

**Ask three classmates the questions below. Write their answers in the chart.**

| Classmate's name: | | | |
|---|---|---|---|
| 1. What is your favorite gadget or machine? | _____ | _____ | _____ |
| 2. How often do you use it? | _____ | _____ | _____ |
| 3. What do you use it for? | _____ | _____ | _____ |
| 4. What other gadget would you like to own? | _____ | _____ | _____ |

Task 2

**Work in groups. Discuss these questions.**

1. What is the most important gadget or machine invented in the last 100 years?
2. What is the most important gadget or machine invented in the last 500 years?
3. What is the most important gadget or machine invented more than 500 years ago?

The printing press

The wheel

The automobile

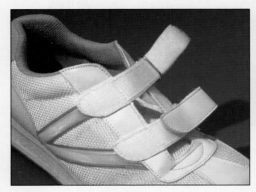
Velcro

The cell phone

The remote control

# UNIT 5 Character Traits

## 1. Getting Ready

How would you describe a good teacher, parent, boss, or friend? Check (✓) your answers and compare them with a partner.

|  | A good teacher | A good parent | A good boss | A good friend |
|---|---|---|---|---|
| intelligent | ☐ | ☐ | ☐ | ☐ |
| strict | ☐ | ☐ | ☐ | ☐ |
| persuasive | ☐ | ☐ | ☐ | ☐ |
| honest | ☐ | ☐ | ☐ | ☐ |
| informed | ☐ | ☐ | ☐ | ☐ |
| enthusiastic | ☐ | ☐ | ☐ | ☐ |
| caring | ☐ | ☐ | ☐ | ☐ |
| sensitive | ☐ | ☐ | ☐ | ☐ |
| patient | ☐ | ☐ | ☐ | ☐ |
| other: _____ | ☐ | ☐ | ☐ | ☐ |

## 2. Let's Listen

People are talking about their friends and classmates. What is each person like? Listen and circle the correct answer.

1. **a.** patient
   **b.** informed

2. **a.** persuasive
   **b.** caring

3. **a.** honest
   **b.** enthusiastic

4. **a.** strict
   **b.** patient

5. **a.** informed
   **b.** sensitive

6. **a.** strict
   **b.** caring

# 3. Let's Listen 💿

Task 1

People are talking about their friends and classmates. Do they praise or criticize the person they talk about? Listen and check (✓) the correct answer.

|    | Praise | Criticize |
|----|--------|-----------|
| 1. | ☐      | ☐         |
| 2. | ☐      | ☐         |
| 3. | ☐      | ☐         |
| 4. | ☐      | ☐         |
| 5. | ☐      | ☐         |
| 6. | ☐      | ☐         |

Task 2

Listen again. Are these statements true or false? Check (✓) the correct answer.

|    |                                                      | True | False |
|----|------------------------------------------------------|------|-------|
| 1. | Chris is informed.                                   | ☐    | ☐     |
|    | Chris is in medical school.                          | ☐    | ☐     |
| 2. | Brandon is caring.                                   | ☐    | ☐     |
|    | Brandon helped the speaker move.                     | ☐    | ☐     |
| 3. | Terry is caring.                                     | ☐    | ☐     |
|    | Terry liked the poor person's clothes.               | ☐    | ☐     |
| 4. | Tony is enthusiastic.                                | ☐    | ☐     |
|    | When Tony is enjoying himself, no one else has fun.  | ☐    | ☐     |
| 5. | Patrick is honest.                                   | ☐    | ☐     |
|    | Patrick wasn't actually sick on the night of the concert. | ☐ | ☐  |
| 6. | Chuck is enthusiastic.                               | ☐    | ☐     |
|    | Chuck isn't going to school this year.               | ☐    | ☐     |

# 4. Let's Listen

## Task 1

People are talking about how their friends have changed. What is each person like now? Listen and check (✓) the correct picture.

1.
a.
b.

2.
a.
b.

3.
a.
b.

4.
a.
b.

## Task 2

Listen again. Are these statements true or false? Check (✓) the correct answer.

|  | True | False |
|---|---|---|
| 1. John is looking for a job. | ☐ | ☐ |
| 2. Donna got married last year. | ☐ | ☐ |
| 3. Rosie broke up with her boyfriend. | ☐ | ☐ |
| 4. Ted lost all his money in the stock market. | ☐ | ☐ |

# Over to You: How have you changed?

**How have you changed in the past five years? Write your answers in the chart and compare them with a partner.**

Example:    A: How do you think you've changed?

B: I used to hate vegetables, but now I eat salad every day. What about you?

|  | Before | Now |
|---|---|---|
| 1. Your hobbies | _____ | _____ |
| 2. Your clothes | _____ | _____ |
| 3. Your likes/dislikes | _____ | _____ |
| 4. Your appearance | _____ | _____ |
| 5. Your personality | _____ | _____ |

**Task 2**

**Imagine it is five years from now. How will you be different than you are today? Write your answers in the chart and compare them with a partner.**

Example:    A: How do you think you will change?

B: Now I wear jeans every day. In the future I'll have a job, so I'll probably wear a suit and tie. What about you?

|  | Now | In the future |
|---|---|---|
| 1. Your hobbies | _____ | _____ |
| 2. Your clothes | _____ | _____ |
| 3. Your likes/dislikes | _____ | _____ |
| 4. Your appearance | _____ | _____ |
| 5. Your personality | _____ | _____ |

# UNIT 6 Cooking

## 1. Getting Ready

**Match the foods on the left with the recipes on the right.**

1. sushi _c_

2. salad ___

3. french fries ___

4. spaghetti ___

5. milk shake ___

a. Cut potatoes into long pieces. Then fry the pieces in hot oil.

b. Boil water and add noodles. Drain the noodles. Then pour sauce on them.

c. Put rice and fresh fish on seaweed. Then roll it together.

d. Put milk in a blender. Add vanilla ice cream, fruit, and sugar. Then blend it together.

e. Chop up some lettuce, carrots, mushrooms, and peppers. Then mix them in a bowl.

## 2. Let's Listen

**People are talking about how to make different kinds of food. Listen and number the pictures.**

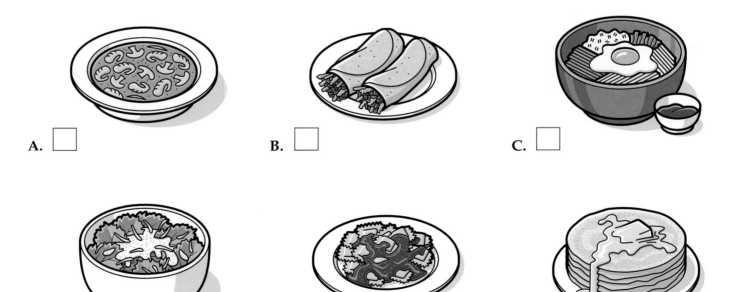

A. ☐

B. ☐

C. ☐

D. ☐

E. ☐

F. ☐

# 3. Let's Listen

## Task 1

The host of a cooking show is explaining how to make crepes. Listen and check (✓) the correct picture.

1.

a.                 b.

2.

a.                 b.

3.

a.                 b.

4.

a.                 b.

## Task 2

Listen again. Are these statements true or false? Check (✓) the correct answer.

|  | True | False |
|---|---|---|
| 1. Milk makes the crepe sweet. | ☐ | ☐ |
| 2. Too much sugar makes the crepe taste awful. | ☐ | ☐ |
| 3. Stir until the liquid is smooth. | ☐ | ☐ |
| 4. Put a lot of butter in the pan. | ☐ | ☐ |

# 4. Let's Listen 💿

People are talking about meals in different countries. Listen and number the pictures.

A. 

B. 

C. 

D. 

E. 

F. | 1 |

Task 2

Listen again. What custom does each person mention? Match the countries on the left with the customs on the right.

1. Taiwan  *b*          a. It's okay to make slurping sounds.

2. Saudi Arabia ___     b. If you see something you like, wave to the waiter.

3. Spain ___            c. Eat with your right hand only.

4. Nepal ___            d. You should eat it late at night.

5. Italy ___            e. Eat everything the host offers you.

6. Japan ___            f. After you're done eating, don't leave right away.

# Over to You: Plan a meal

Do you know these foods and ingredients? Write the names below each picture.

| | | | | | |
|---|---|---|---|---|---|
| rice | onions | noodles | salt and pepper | tomatoes | milk |
| sugar | fish | soy sauce | eggs | garlic | peaches |

1. _____rice_____    2. _____    3. _____    4. _____

5. _____    6. _____    7. _____    8. _____

9. _____    10. _____    11. _____    12. _____

Task 2

Work in groups. Plan a meal using all of the foods and ingredients above.
Write your recipes on a piece of paper.

# UNIT 7 Housing

## 1. Getting Ready

Which kind of housing would you prefer? Number the items from 1 (your favorite) to 6 (your least favorite). Compare your answers with a partner.

**Favorite housing**

___ a large apartment in the suburbs

___ a house in the suburbs with a large yard

___ a house in the city with a garage

___ a house in the country

___ a studio apartment in the city

___ other: _____

## 2. Let's Listen

People are talking about housing. What kind of house or apartment does each person need? Listen and circle the correct answer.

1. a. a studio apartment
   b. a three bedroom apartment

2. a. an apartment in the city
   b. a house with a yard

3. a. an apartment in the city
   b. a house in the suburbs

4. a. a house in the country
   b. a house in the city

5. a. a large apartment
   b. a one bedroom apartment

6. a. a small apartment in the city
   b. a small apartment near the airport

# 3. Let's Listen

Task 1

**People are talking about where they live. What do the people dislike about each place? Listen and circle the correct answer.**

1. **a.** location
   **b.** condition
   **c.** rent

2. **a.** neighbors
   **b.** noise
   **c.** size

3. **a.** location
   **b.** noise
   **c.** size

4. **a.** size
   **b.** location
   **c.** rent

5. **a.** size
   **b.** condition
   **c.** noise

6. **a.** neighbors
   **b.** condition
   **c.** rent

Task 2

**Listen again. What do the people like about each place?
Write the correct letter.**

1. ___          **a.** It's huge.

2. ___          **b.** The rent is much cheaper.

3. ___          **c.** It's convenient for shopping.

4. ___          **d.** It's nice and quiet on the weekends.

5. ___          **e.** The neighbors are fantastic.

6. ___          **f.** The location is perfect.

# 4. Let's Listen

Task 1

People are talking about why they moved to a different place. Does the information in the chart describe their old place or their new place? Check (✓) the correct answer.

| | Old place | New place |
|---|:---:|:---:|
| **1.** loud neighbors | ✓ | ☐ |
| quiet neighbors | ☐ | ☐ |
| **2.** no noise at all | ☐ | ☐ |
| traffic noise | ☐ | ☐ |
| **3.** wonderful landlady | ☐ | ☐ |
| close to a good school | ☐ | ☐ |
| **4.** no pets allowed | ☐ | ☐ |
| near a park | ☐ | ☐ |
| **5.** great stove | ☐ | ☐ |
| small dining room | ☐ | ☐ |
| **6.** expensive to take care of | ☐ | ☐ |
| a lot cheaper | ☐ | ☐ |

Task 2

Listen again. What kind of place do they live in now? Circle the correct answer.

**1.** **a.** an apartment downtown
  **b.** a house in the suburbs
  **c.** a studio apartment

**2.** **a.** a house in the country
  **b.** an apartment on a high floor
  **c.** an apartment on the first floor

**3.** **a.** an apartment in the city
  **b.** an apartment in the suburbs
  **c.** a house in the country

**4.** **a.** a building near the park
  **b.** an apartment downtown
  **c.** a house in the suburbs

**5.** **a.** a house in the city
  **b.** an apartment with no kitchen
  **c.** an apartment with a huge kitchen

**6.** **a.** an apartment with no yard
  **b.** a house with a yard
  **c.** a house with no yard

# Over to You: Your dream house

Task 1

**Work in pairs. Design your dream house. Discuss these questions.**

1. Where will it be?

2. How many rooms will it have?

3. Will it have any of these special features?
   - a swimming pool
   - a hot tub
   - a sauna
   - a tennis court
   - a large garden

Task 2

**Work in pairs. Draw your dream house.**

Task 3

**Work in groups. Describe your dream house to your group members.**

# UNIT 8 Apartment Problems

## 1. Getting Ready

**Match the apartment problems on the left with the solutions on the right.**

1. The hallways are too dark. _d_

2. The garbage is not picked up on time. ___

3. The neighbors are noisy. ___

4. There are too many door-to-door salespeople. ___

5. The roof leaks. ___

  **a.** Put a sign in the lobby.

  **b.** Talk to the landlord.

  **c.** Contact the local sanitation department.

  **d.** Replace the lights more often.

  **e.** Speak to the neighbors.

## 2. Let's Listen

**People are talking about problems with their apartments. What problems do they describe? Listen and circle the correct answer.**

1. **a.** The walls are too thin.
   **b.** The TV reception is poor.

2. **a.** The neighbor is noisy.
   **b.** The roof leaks.

3. **a.** The garbage is picked up too early.
   **b.** The hallways are too dark.

4. **a.** There are too many ads in the mailboxes.
   **b.** There are too many salespeople.

5. **a.** The kitchen appliances are too old.
   **b.** The bathroom appliances are too old.

6. **a.** The neighbor is noisy.
   **b.** The neighbor's dog makes a mess.

# 3. Let's Listen

## Task 1

A person is talking about problems with an apartment. Listen and write the correct letter in the chart.

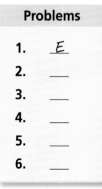

| Problems |
|---|
| 1. _E_ |
| 2. __ |
| 3. __ |
| 4. __ |
| 5. __ |
| 6. __ |

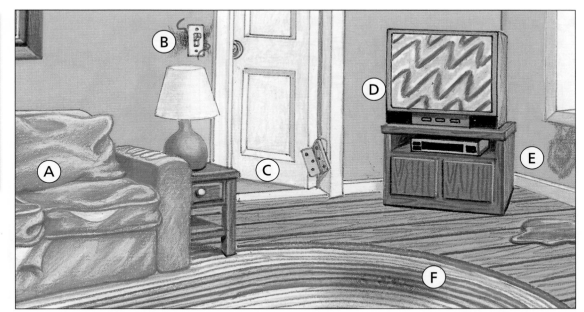

## Task 2

Listen again. What is the problem with each item? Circle the correct answer.

1. a. It really needs cleaning.
   b. It really needs painting.
   c. It really needs replacing.

2. a. It's much too big.
   b. The smell is horrible.
   c. The color is horrible.

3. a. It doesn't work.
   b. It's too dangerous.
   c. It isn't the right color.

4. a. It doesn't open easily.
   b. It's falling off.
   c. It needs a new coat of paint.

5. a. It isn't very comfortable.
   b. It's really worn thin.
   c. It makes a noise when you sit down.

6. a. The screen is too small.
   b. It doesn't make any sound.
   c. The reception is very bad.

# 4. Let's Listen 💿

People are complaining to their landlord. What problem does each person have?
Listen and circle the correct answer.

1. a. There are too many ads in the mailboxes.
   b. There are too many salespeople.
   c. The neighbors are noisy.

2. a. The kitchen is dirty.
   b. The living room needs painting.
   c. The walls are too thin.

3. a. The window is broken.
   b. The TV reception is poor.
   c. The neighbors are noisy.

4. a. The roof leaks.
   b. The kitchen needs repainting.
   c. The refrigerator is too old.

5. a. The faucet leaks.
   b. The roof leaks.
   c. The neighbors are noisy.

6. a. The sofa needs replacing.
   b. The curtains are worn out.
   c. The walls are too thin.

**Task 2**

Listen again. Does the landlord agree to help the people? Check (✓) the
correct answer.

|    | Agrees | Doesn't agree |
|----|--------|---------------|
| 1. | ☐ | ☐ |
| 2. | ☐ | ☐ |
| 3. | ☐ | ☐ |
| 4. | ☐ | ☐ |
| 5. | ☐ | ☐ |
| 6. | ☐ | ☐ |

# Over to You: What seems to be the problem?

**What are some common apartment problems? Write five more problems.**

1. *The refrigerator is broken.*
2. _____
3. _____
4. _____
5. _____
6. _____

**Task 2**

**Work in pairs. Student A is a tenant with a problem. Student B is a landlord. Practice the conversation below.**

**A:** Hi, this is (1) <u>Yuko</u> from (2) <u>apartment 4C</u>.

**B:** Oh, hi. What seems to be the problem?

**A:** (3) <u>The refrigerator is broken</u>. Can you (4) <u>fix it</u>?

**B:** (5) <u>Sure. I'll send someone right away.</u>

**Task 3**

**Work in pairs. Have two more conversations like the one in Task 2. Use this information.**

| | |
|---|---|
| (1) Tommy | Wendy |
| (2) 1804 | the third floor |
| (3) The neighbors are too noisy. | The toilet is broken. |
| (4) ask them to be quiet? | call a plumber right away? |
| (5) Okay. I'll call them. | Sorry, I can't until next week. |

**Task 4**

**Work in pairs. Take turns role-playing the situation in Task 2. Use your own information.**

# UNIT 9 Friendship

## 1. Getting Ready

What do you think are the most important qualities in a friend?
Check (✓) your answers and compare them with a partner.

|  | Very important | Somewhat important | Not important |
|---|---|---|---|
| appearance | ☐ | ☐ | ☐ |
| family background | ☐ | ☐ | ☐ |
| education | ☐ | ☐ | ☐ |
| sense of humor | ☐ | ☐ | ☐ |
| intelligence | ☐ | ☐ | ☐ |
| career goals | ☐ | ☐ | ☐ |
| sensitivity | ☐ | ☐ | ☐ |
| social skills | ☐ | ☐ | ☐ |
| other: _____ | ☐ | ☐ | ☐ |

## 2. Let's Listen 💿

People are describing their friends. What qualities are they talking about?
Listen and circle the correct answer.

1. **a.** sense of humor
   **b.** sensitivity

2. **a.** family background
   **b.** career goals

3. **a.** social skills
   **b.** sense of humor

4. **a.** education
   **b.** family background

5. **a.** appearance
   **b.** intelligence

6. **a.** sense of humor
   **b.** appearance

# 3. Let's Listen

Task 1

**People are giving invitations. Listen and number the pictures.**

A.

B.

C.

D.

E.

F.

Task 2

**Listen again. Circle the correct information about each invitation.**

1. a. Lynne refuses Dave's invitation.
   b. The invitation is for Saturday.
   c. Lynne will meet Dave's parents on Saturday.

2. a. Paula already has plans.
   b. They will meet at the bookstore.
   c. The invitation is for Friday.

3. a. There will be free drinks and food.
   b. Rose refuses the invitation.
   c. Rose doesn't think it will be fun.

4. a. Ron accepts the invitation.
   b. Ron has to study for a big exam.
   c. Ron has to work late.

5. a. They will go downtown after class.
   b. They both hate listening to music.
   c. The invitation is for next month.

6. a. The invitation is for Sunday.
   b. George likes those kinds of shows.
   c. They will go to the show in the morning.

# 4. Let's Listen

**Task 1**

**People are giving invitations. What events are they talking about?**
**Listen and circle the correct answer.**

1. **a.** art show
   **b.** sports festival
   **c.** children's concert

2. **a.** craft fair
   **b.** food fair
   **c.** farm show

3. **a.** movie premiere
   **b.** restaurant opening
   **c.** ice-skating exhibition

4. **a.** restaurant opening
   **b.** book signing
   **c.** fashion show

5. **a.** car race
   **b.** football game
   **c.** marathon

6. **a.** flower show
   **b.** art show
   **c.** concert

**Task 2**

**Listen again. What reason does each person give for refusing the invitation?**
**Write the correct letter.**

1. He ___          **a.** hates big crowds.

2. She ___         **b.** thinks the writer's books are boring.

3. She ___         **c.** heard it's going to be cold.

4. He ___          **d.** was planning to watch TV.

5. She ___         **e.** just started a new diet.

6. She ___         **f.** is only interested in famous artists.

# Over to You: Would you like to ...?

**What are some things people do on the weekend? Write five more activities.**

1. *go to a baseball game*
2. _____
3. _____
4. _____
5. _____
6. _____

**Task 2**

**Move around the class and invite three people to one of the activities on your list. Write their answers in the chart.**

**Example:** **A:** Hey, Debbie, would you like to go to a baseball game on Saturday?

**B:** Sorry, I can't. I already have plans for Saturday.

**A:** Oh, well. Maybe another time.

| | Name | Accept | Refuse | Reason |
|---|---|---|---|---|
| 1. | *Debbie* | ☐ | ☑ | *She already has plans.* |
| 2. | _____ | ☐ | ☐ | _____ |
| 3. | _____ | ☐ | ☐ | _____ |
| 4. | _____ | ☐ | ☐ | _____ |

# UNIT 10 Television

## 1. Getting Ready

How often do you watch these kinds of TV programs? Check (✓) your answers and compare them with a partner.

|  | Often | Sometimes | Rarely | Never |
|---|---|---|---|---|
| sports | ☐ | ☐ | ☐ | ☐ |
| documentaries | ☐ | ☐ | ☐ | ☐ |
| sitcoms | ☐ | ☐ | ☐ | ☐ |
| game shows | ☐ | ☐ | ☐ | ☐ |
| news programs | ☐ | ☐ | ☐ | ☐ |
| movies | ☐ | ☐ | ☐ | ☐ |
| reality shows | ☐ | ☐ | ☐ | ☐ |
| soap operas | ☐ | ☐ | ☐ | ☐ |
| talk shows | ☐ | ☐ | ☐ | ☐ |
| other: _____ | ☐ | ☐ | ☐ | ☐ |

## 2. Let's Listen

People are talking about TV. What kind of program did each person watch? Listen and circle the correct answer.

1. a. soap opera
   b. movie

2. a. game show
   b. sitcom

3. a. sports
   b. documentary

4. a. sitcom
   b. news

5. a. sports
   b. soap opera

6. a. sitcom
   b. documentary

# 3. Let's Listen

Announcers are talking about tonight's television programs. Listen and write the correct number in the TV program guide.

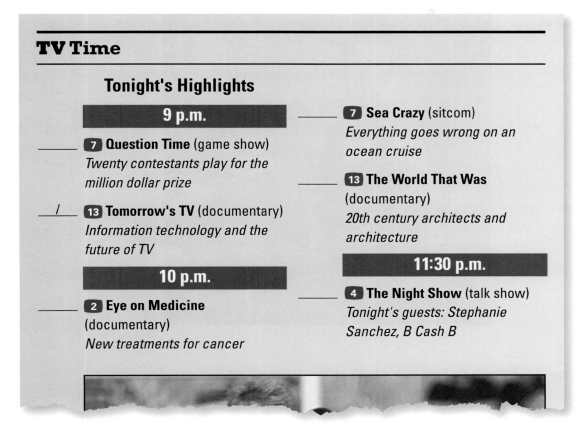

**TV Time**

**Tonight's Highlights**

**9 p.m.**

_____ **7 Question Time** (game show)
*Twenty contestants play for the million dollar prize*

__/__ **13 Tomorrow's TV** (documentary)
*Information technology and the future of TV*

**10 p.m.**

_____ **2 Eye on Medicine** (documentary)
*New treatments for cancer*

_____ **7 Sea Crazy** (sitcom)
*Everything goes wrong on an ocean cruise*

_____ **13 The World That Was** (documentary)
*20th century architects and architecture*

**11:30 p.m.**

_____ **4 The Night Show** (talk show)
*Tonight's guests: Stephanie Sanchez, B Cash B*

**Task 2**

Listen again. Who will probably want to watch these programs?
Write the correct letter.

1. ___     a. people interested in architecture

2. ___     b. people who are thinking of taking a cruise

3. ___     c. people who love technology

4. ___     d. people who love movies and music

5. ___     e. people who love facts and trivia

6. ___     f. people over 40

# 4. Let's Listen

**Task 1**

People are giving their opinions about TV programs. Do they agree?
Listen and check (✓) the correct answer.

| | Agree | Don't agree |
|---|---|---|
| 1. | ✓ | ☐ |
| 2. | ☐ | ☐ |
| 3. | ☐ | ☐ |
| 4. | ☐ | ☐ |
| 5. | ☐ | ☐ |
| 6. | ☐ | ☐ |

**Task 2**

Listen again. Are these statements true or false? Check (✓) the correct answer.

| | True | False |
|---|---|---|
| 1. She thinks the recipes are difficult. | ☐ | ☐ |
| 2. She loves figuring out how magicians do their tricks. | ☐ | ☐ |
| 3. He would rather play tennis than watch it. | ☐ | ☐ |
| 4. She thinks the photography is amazing. | ☐ | ☐ |
| 5. He would rather watch a show about an expensive hotel. | ☐ | ☐ |
| 6. She would rather watch sports. | ☐ | ☐ |

# Over to You: What are your favorite programs?

What programs are on television these days? Write six titles and compare them with a partner.

1. _____

2. _____

3. _____

4. _____

5. _____

6. _____

Task 2

What are your favorite and least favorite programs on television, and why? Write your answers in the chart and compare them with a partner.

Example:   **A:** What are your favorite programs?

**B:** My favorite programs are…

**A:** Why's that?

**B:** Well, because…

| Favorite programs | Reasons |
|---|---|
| 1. _____ | _____ |
| 2. _____ | _____ |
| 3. _____ | _____ |

| Least favorite programs | Reasons |
|---|---|
| 1. _____ | _____ |
| 2. _____ | _____ |
| 3. _____ | _____ |

# UNIT 11 Cities

## 1. Getting Ready

**What cities are famous for these things? Write your answers in the chart and compare them with a partner.**

| Feature | City |
|---|---|
| nightlife | _____ |
| traffic | _____ |
| shopping | _____ |
| culture | _____ |
| safety | _____ |
| architecture | _____ |
| beaches | _____ |
| other: _____ | _____ |

## 2. Let's Listen

**People are talking about different cities. What do they like about each city? Listen and circle the correct answer.**

1. **a.** nightlife
   **b.** safety

2. **a.** architecture
   **b.** weather

3. **a.** weather
   **b.** nightlife

4. **a.** culture
   **b.** pollution

5. **a.** prices
   **b.** beaches

6. **a.** traffic
   **b.** sightseeing

# 3. Let's Listen

Task 1

Dave is asking his friend about Quebec province in Canada. Are these statements about Quebec City or Montreal? Listen and check (✓) the correct answer.

|  | Quebec City | Montreal |
|---|:---:|:---:|
| 1. It's the biggest city in Quebec province. | ☐ | ☑ |
| 2. It's the capital of the province. | ☐ | ☐ |
| 3. The St. Lawrence River runs through it. | ☐ | ☐ |
| 4. It's the third-largest French-speaking city in the world. | ☐ | ☐ |
| 5. Many of the buildings are very old. | ☐ | ☐ |

Task 2

Listen again and answer the questions. Circle the correct answer.

1. Why is Dave going to Quebec?

   a. to get married
   b. for a friend's wedding
   c. for a job

2. How long will he be in Montreal?

   a. a week
   b. two days
   c. four days

3. How is Dave's French?

   a. perfect
   b. okay, but not great
   c. very bad

4. Who is Dave going to visit in Quebec City?

   a. a friend from college
   b. his uncle
   c. his teacher

# 4. Let's Listen

Task 1

People are talking about good experiences they had in different cities.
What happened to each person? Listen and circle the correct answer.

1. a. She didn't have to speak any Spanish.
   b. She spoke Spanish every day.

2. a. The taxi driver gave her a free ride.
   b. The taxi driver returned her wallet.

3. a. He met a Greek family on the boat.
   b. He stayed in a great hotel.

4. a. She went snorkeling.
   b. She ate some fantastic fish.

5. a. He saw a famous actor in a restaurant.
   b. He went to the theater often.

6. a. She went to Tokyo Disneyland.
   b. The weather was great.

Task 2

Listen again. Are these statements true or false? Check (✓) the correct answer.

|  | True | False |
|---|---|---|
| 1. Someone stole her lunch. | ☐ | ☐ |
| 2. She got food poisoning from seafood. | ☐ | ☐ |
| 3. He had to sleep at the bus station. | ☐ | ☐ |
| 4. She got a great suntan. | ☐ | ☐ |
| 5. He ran out of money. | ☐ | ☐ |
| 6. She brought too much warm clothing. | ☐ | ☐ |

# Over to You: True or false?

Task 1

Work in groups. Write three true statements about a city or country that your group knows. Then write two false statements.

Examples: **True:**  Hong Kong is a city in Asia.

**False:**  More than 20 million people live in Hong Kong.

| True | False |
|------|-------|
| 1. _____ _____ | 1. _____ _____ |
| 2. _____ _____ | 2. _____ _____ |
| 3. _____ _____ | |

Task 2

Work in pairs. Take turns reading your statements aloud and guessing which ones are true or false.

Task 3

Write true and false statements about your hometown on a piece of paper. Then find a new partner. Take turns reading the statements aloud and guessing which ones are true or false.

# UNIT 12 Urban Life

## 1. Getting Ready

How do you like your town or city? Check (✓) your answers and compare them with a partner.

|  | Like it a lot | Like it a little | Don't like it |
|---|:---:|:---:|:---:|
| parks | ☐ | ☐ | ☐ |
| public transportation | ☐ | ☐ | ☐ |
| nightlife | ☐ | ☐ | ☐ |
| restaurants | ☐ | ☐ | ☐ |
| air quality | ☐ | ☐ | ☐ |
| safety | ☐ | ☐ | ☐ |
| traffic | ☐ | ☐ | ☐ |
| cleanliness | ☐ | ☐ | ☐ |
| the economy | ☐ | ☐ | ☐ |
| other: _____ | ☐ | ☐ | ☐ |

## 2. Let's Listen 💿

People are describing the cities where they live. What topic are they talking about? Circle the correct answer.

1. a. the economy
   b. traffic

2. a. safety
   b. shopping

3. a. parks
   b. public transportation

4. a. the economy
   b. cleanliness

5. a. safety
   b. restaurants

6. a. noise
   b. air quality

# 3. Let's Listen

## Task 1

People are talking about how their cities have changed. What is each city like now? Listen and check (✓) the correct picture.

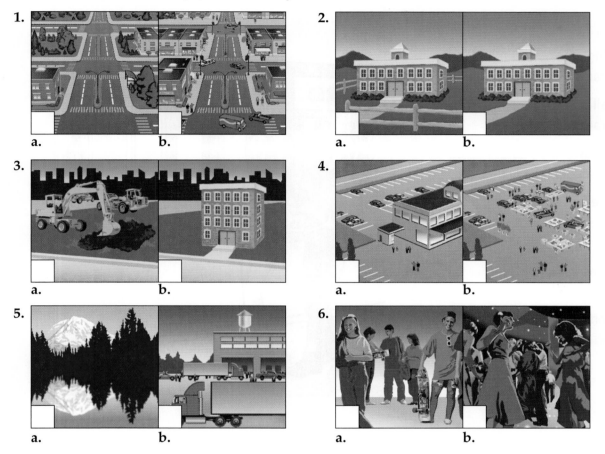

1. a.     b.
2. a.     b.
3. a.     b.
4. a.     b.
5. a.     b.
6. a.     b.

## Task 2

Listen again. Are these statements true or false? Check (✓) the correct answer.

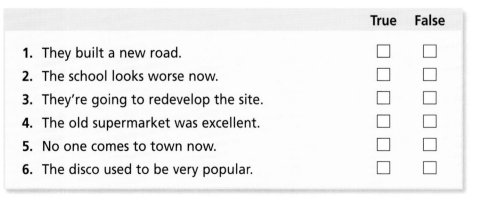

|  | True | False |
|---|---|---|
| 1. They built a new road. | ☐ | ☐ |
| 2. The school looks worse now. | ☐ | ☐ |
| 3. They're going to redevelop the site. | ☐ | ☐ |
| 4. The old supermarket was excellent. | ☐ | ☐ |
| 5. No one comes to town now. | ☐ | ☐ |
| 6. The disco used to be very popular. | ☐ | ☐ |

# 4. Let's Listen 💿

Task 1

People are talking about the cities where they live. What do they like about living there? What do they dislike? Listen and check (✓) the correct answers.

|   |  | Likes | Dislikes |
|---|---|:---:|:---:|
| 1. | shopping | ☑ | ☐ |
|   | restaurants | ☐ | ☐ |
| 2. | the mall | ☐ | ☐ |
|   | restaurants | ☐ | ☐ |
| 3. | cleanliness | ☐ | ☐ |
|   | parks | ☐ | ☐ |
| 4. | nightlife | ☐ | ☐ |
|   | safety | ☐ | ☐ |
| 5. | traffic | ☐ | ☐ |
|   | the subway | ☐ | ☐ |
| 6. | air quality | ☐ | ☐ |
|   | the economy | ☐ | ☐ |

Task 2

Listen again. What changes or improvements do the people suggest for each city? Write the correct letter.

1. ___       a. bring more businesses here

2. ___       b. build new highways

3. ___       c. open some clubs or discos

4. ___       d. build more parks downtown

5. ___       e. open a restaurant that serves seafood

6. ___       f. have a few cheap stores

# Over to You: Improving your city

**Work in groups. What improvements need to be made to these features of your town or city? Why? Write your group's ideas in the chart.**

Example:   **A:** How can we improve air quality?

             **B:** I think we should build roads for bicycles.

             **C:** Why is that?

             **A:** Because more people will ride bicycles to work instead of driving their cars.

|  | Improvements |
|---|---|
| **1.** air quality | *build roads for bicycles* |
| **2.** nightlife | |
| **3.** public transportation | |
| **4.** restaurants | |
| **5.** the economy | |

**Task 2**

**Work in pairs. Compare your ideas from Task 1 with your partner. Make a list of the five most important improvements needed in your town or city.**

| | Improvements |
|---|---|
| **1.** | |
| **2.** | |
| **3.** | |
| **4.** | |
| **5.** | |

# UNIT 13 Special Days

## 1. Getting Ready

**Match the special days on the left with the descriptions on the right.**

1. Valentine's Day _d_
2. April Fool's Day ___
3. Halloween ___
4. Children's Day ___

   a. People like to play tricks on their friends on this day.

   b. Adults honor kids on this day and do special things with them.

   c. Children dress up in strange costumes on this day.

   d. People give cards, candy, or flowers to their friends and loved ones on this day.

## 2. Let's Listen

**People are describing holidays and special events. Listen and number the pictures.**

A.

B.

C.

D.

E.

F.

# 3. Let's Listen

## Task 1

People are talking about how they celebrate their birthdays. Do they stay home or go out? Check (✓) the correct answer.

| | Stays home | Goes out |
|---|---|---|
| 1. | ☐ | ☐ |
| 2. | ☐ | ☐ |
| 3. | ☐ | ☐ |
| 4. | ☐ | ☐ |
| 5. | ☐ | ☐ |
| 6. | ☐ | ☐ |

## Task 2

Listen again. What do the people do on their birthdays now? Circle the correct answer.

1. **a.** go to a restaurant
   **b.** eat cake
   **c.** have a party

2. **a.** go to school
   **b.** go dancing
   **c.** come home early

3. **a.** go to a restaurant
   **b.** open presents
   **c.** eat cake

4. **a.** have a party
   **b.** go dancing
   **c.** watch a video

5. **a.** go to a friend's house
   **b.** have a party
   **c.** spend time with parents

6. **a.** go to a movie
   **b.** go out to dinner
   **c.** receive a present

## 4. Let's Listen

**Task 1**

People are talking about special days. Do they like each day?
Check (✓) the correct answer.

|  |  | Likes | Doesn't like |
|---|---|:---:|:---:|
| 1. | Valentine's Day | ✓ | ☐ |
| 2. | April Fool's Day | ☐ | ☐ |
| 3. | Christmas | ☐ | ☐ |
| 4. | Halloween | ☐ | ☐ |
| 5. | Christmas | ☐ | ☐ |
| 6. | New Year's Eve | ☐ | ☐ |

## 4. Let's Listen

**Task 1**

1. **a.** She didn't get any valentines.
   **b.** She got a real valentine.
   **c.** She broke up with her boyfriend.

2. **a.** His co-worker played a trick on him.
   **b.** He had a wonderful time.
   **c.** He played tricks on all his friends.

3. **a.** He didn't buy any presents.
   **b.** He received an expensive gift.
   **c.** He gave money to charity.

4. **a.** Her kids went to a party.
   **b.** Her kids went to strangers' houses.
   **c.** Her kids studied for a test.

5. **a.** He spent Christmas alone.
   **b.** He had a party with his friends.
   **c.** He had a big family dinner.

6. **a.** She went to a great party.
   **b.** She went dancing.
   **c.** The neighbors had a noisy party.

# Over to You: Your best holiday experience

Task 1

Think of the best time you've ever had on a holiday or special day. Write questions you'd like someone to ask you about your experience.

Examples:  What holiday was it?

How old were you?

Where did you go?

Did you get a present?

What did you eat?

| Questions |
|---|
| 1. _____ |
| 2. _____ |
| 3. _____ |
| 4. _____ |
| 5. _____ |

Task 2

Work in pairs. Switch books with your partner. Ask him or her the questions written in the chart. Then ask your partner three more questions about his or her experience.

Task 3

Work in groups. Tell your group about your partner's experience.

## 1. Getting Ready

What clothes do you usually wear to these places or events?
Complete the chart and compare your answers with a partner.

|  | Formal | Informal | Clothing |
|---|---|---|---|
| a wedding | ☐ | ☐ | _____ |
| work | ☐ | ☐ | _____ |
| a party | ☐ | ☐ | _____ |
| school | ☐ | ☐ | _____ |
| other: _____ | ☐ | ☐ | _____ |

## 2. Let's Listen 💿

People are talking about fashions from the past. Listen and number the pictures.

A.

B.

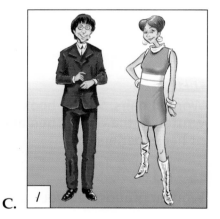

C. | / |

D.

E.

F.

# 3. Let's Listen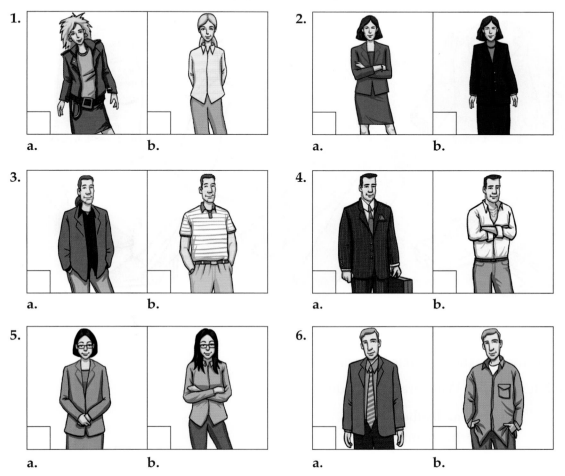

**Task 1**

People are talking about how their friends have changed. What do their friends look like now? Listen and check (✓) the correct picture.

1.
a.    b.

2.
a.    b.

3.
a.    b.

4.
a.    b.

5.
a.    b.

6.
a.    b.

**Task 2**

Listen again. Are these statements true or false? Check (✓) the correct answer.

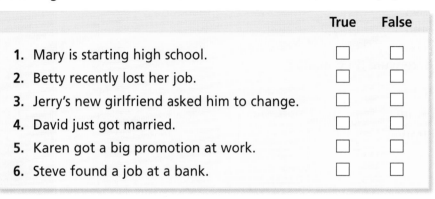

|  | True | False |
|---|---|---|
| **1.** Mary is starting high school. | ☐ | ☐ |
| **2.** Betty recently lost her job. | ☐ | ☐ |
| **3.** Jerry's new girlfriend asked him to change. | ☐ | ☐ |
| **4.** David just got married. | ☐ | ☐ |
| **5.** Karen got a big promotion at work. | ☐ | ☐ |
| **6.** Steve found a job at a bank. | ☐ | ☐ |

# 4. Let's Listen 💿

Task 1

People are describing things they have just bought. Listen and write the correct letter in the chart.

| Items |
| --- |
| 1. _F_ |
| 2. __ |
| 3. __ |
| 4. __ |
| 5. __ |
| 6. __ |

Task 2

Listen again and answer the questions. Circle the correct answer.

1. Where were they made?

   a. Italy
   b. China
   c. the U.S.

2. What is it made of?

   a. cotton
   b. leather
   c. wool

3. How much did it cost?

   a. $50
   b. $100
   c. $200

4. What are they made of?

   a. leather
   b. denim
   c. silk

5. How much did it cost?

   a. $90
   b. $95
   c. $99

6. Where were they made?

   a. China
   b. Korea
   c. Italy

# Over to You: What looks good on you?

Task 1

What looks good on you? Write your answers in the chart
and compare them with a partner.

Example:     **A:** What clothes look good on you?

                **B:** A suit looks good on me, because it makes me look older and
                     more experienced. What clothes look good on you?

|  | You | Your partner |
|---|---|---|
| 1. clothes that look good on me | _____ | _____ |
| 2. clothes that don't look good on me | _____ | _____ |
| 3. colors that look good on me | _____ | _____ |
| 4. colors that don't look good on me | _____ | _____ |
| 5. styles that look good on me | _____ | _____ |
| 6. styles that don't look good on me | _____ | _____ |

Task 2

**Work in pairs. Suggest new clothes for your partner. Use the information
from Task 1.**

# UNIT 15 Preferences

## 1. Getting Ready

What kinds of things do you like? Write your answers in the chart and
compare them with a partner.

|  | You | Your partner |
| --- | --- | --- |
| favorite kind of movie | _____ | _____ |
| favorite kind of music | _____ | _____ |
| favorite kind of food | _____ | _____ |
| favorite sport | _____ | _____ |
| favorite free time activity | _____ | _____ |
| other: _____ | _____ | _____ |

## 2. Let's Listen

People are talking about their preferences. What do they prefer?
Listen and circle the correct answer.

1. a. traveling by plane
   b. traveling by train

2. a. living in an apartment
   b. living in a house

3. a. British English
   b. American English

4. a. working in an office
   b. working in a store

5. a. learning Spanish
   b. learning German

6. a. country-western music
   b. rock music

# 3. Let's Listen

## Task 1

People are talking about things they like. Listen and number the pictures.

A.

B. /

C.

D.

E.

F.

## Task 2

Listen again. Do the people agree? Check (✓) the correct answer.

1. ☐ agree
   ☐ don't agree

2. ☐ agree
   ☐ don't agree

3. ☐ agree
   ☐ don't agree

4. ☐ agree
   ☐ don't agree

5. ☐ agree
   ☐ don't agree

6. ☐ agree
   ☐ don't agree

# 4. Let's Listen

**Task 1**

People are giving their preferences. What topic is each person talking about?
Listen and circle the correct answer.

1. **a.** vacations
   **b.** friends
   **c.** exercise

2. **a.** stores
   **b.** restaurants
   **c.** places to live

3. **a.** hotels
   **b.** places to live
   **c.** schools

4. **a.** cars
   **b.** hotels
   **c.** places to live

5. **a.** cars
   **b.** computers
   **c.** dogs

6. **a.** vacations
   **b.** jobs
   **c.** sports

**Task 2**

Listen again. Are these statements true or false? Check (✓) the correct answer.

|  | True | False |
|---|:---:|:---:|
| 1. He prefers traveling by himself. | ☐ | ☐ |
| 2. She likes those loud, trendy places. | ☐ | ☐ |
| 3. She likes places with a swimming pool. | ☐ | ☐ |
| 4. He can't stand living in the suburbs. | ☐ | ☐ |
| 5. She wants a small one that she can carry. | ☐ | ☐ |
| 6. Making a lot of money isn't important to him. | ☐ | ☐ |

# Over to You: What do you prefer?

## Task 1

Write three questions about preferences.

| Questions |
|---|
| 1. *Do you prefer rock music or reggae?* |
| 2. |
| 3. |
| 4. |

## Task 2

Move around the class. Ask three people about their preferences.
Ask each person the reason for each preference.

**Example:** **A:** John, do you prefer rock music or reggae?

**B:** I prefer rock music.

**A:** Why?

**B:** Because I like the sound of guitars.

| | Name | Preference | Reason |
|---|---|---|---|
| 1. | *John* | *rock music* | *He likes the sound of guitars.* |
| 2. | | | |
| 3. | | | |
| 4. | | | |

# UNIT 16 Phone Messages

## 1. Getting Ready

**Match the callers on the left with the messages on the right.**

1. Pete's Garage called _b_
2. Tony and Sue called ___
3. The travel agent called ___
4. The dentist's office called ___

a. to confirm your flight on Friday.
b. to say the estimate for repairs is $475.
c. to invite you to a party on Saturday.
d. to remind you of an appointment.

## 2. Let's Listen

**People are leaving phone messages. What kinds of messages are they?
Listen and circle the correct answer.**

1. a. congratulations
   b. a suggestion

2. a. an invitation
   b. an apology

3. a. an offer
   b. a reminder

4. a. a request
   b. an apology

5. a. a reminder
   b. a suggestion

6. a. an invitation
   b. congratulations

# 3. Let's Listen 📀

**Task 1**

People are leaving phone messages. Listen and number the pictures.

A.

B.

C.

D.

E.

F.

**Task 2**

Listen again. How does each caller sound? Circle the correct answer.

1. Louise sounds _____.

   a. pleased
   b. angry
   c. apologetic

2. Mr. Norris sounds _____.

   a. scared
   b. apologetic
   c. excited

3. Anne sounds _____.

   a. apologetic
   b. worried
   c. pleased

4. Mr. Grant sounds _____.

   a. angry
   b. bored
   c. apologetic

5. Judy Peterson sounds _____.

   a. excited
   b. angry
   c. worried

6. Mrs. Brown sounds _____.

   a. apologetic
   b. scared
   c. angry

# 4. Let's Listen

People are leaving phone messages. Listen and correct the mistakes in each message.

1.
**WHILE YOU WERE OUT**

To: Pamela Gordon
From: Ken Moore
Phone Number: 834-6627
Message: Your flight on Tuesday now leaves at 10:30, not 9:45.

2.
**WHILE YOU WERE OUT**

To: Jane Taylor
From: Brian from the bank
Phone Number: 447-7316
Message: The book you ordered will be in next week.

3.
**WHILE YOU WERE OUT**

To: Mr. Garcia
From: Jeff Lee
Phone Number: 627-6002
Message: He will be late to Spanish class tonight.

4.
**WHILE YOU WERE OUT**

To: Benny
From: Rosie White from Pet World
Phone Number: 867-5539
Message: You can come on Sunday morning at 11 a.m.

Task 2

Listen again. Where is each person the caller asks for? Circle the correct answer.

1. a. at lunch
   b. at a meeting
   c. on vacation

2. a. at a meeting
   b. at home
   c. at lunch

3. a. in class
   b. at lunch
   c. at home

4. a. on vacation
   b. at the mall
   c. at the bank

# Over to You: Leave your own message

**Work in pairs. Give these messages to different classmates. Complete the message pads and then read them to your classmates.**

## WHILE YOU WERE OUT

To:

From: Your mother

Message: She wants you to

Telephoned ✓ | Returned your call ☐ | Will call again ☐

Wants to see you: ☐ | Please call back: ☐ | Came in: ☐

## WHILE YOU WERE OUT

To:

From: Police Officer Daniels

Message: Call immediately because

Telephoned ☐ | Returned your call ☐ | Will call again ☐

Wants to see you: ☐ | Please call back: ☐ | Came in: ☐

## WHILE YOU WERE OUT

To:

From: Carmen

Message: called from Los Angeles and said

Telephoned ☐ | Returned your call ☐ | Will call again ☐

Wants to see you: ☐ | Please call back: ☐ | Came in: ☐

## WHILE YOU WERE OUT

To:

From: A man

Message: He wouldn't leave his name but he said to tell you

Telephoned ☐ | Returned your call ☐ | Will call again ☐

Wants to see you: ☐ | Please call back: ☐ | Came in: ☐

# UNIT 17 Past Events

## 1. Getting Ready

Have any of these things ever happened to you? Check (✓) your answers and compare them with a partner.

|  |  | Yes | No |
|---|---|---|---|
| 1. | You locked yourself out of your home. | ☐ | ☐ |
| 2. | You had a bad experience while flying. | ☐ | ☐ |
| 3. | You were in a traffic accident. | ☐ | ☐ |
| 4. | You got stuck in an elevator. | ☐ | ☐ |
| 5. | You found something valuable on the street. | ☐ | ☐ |

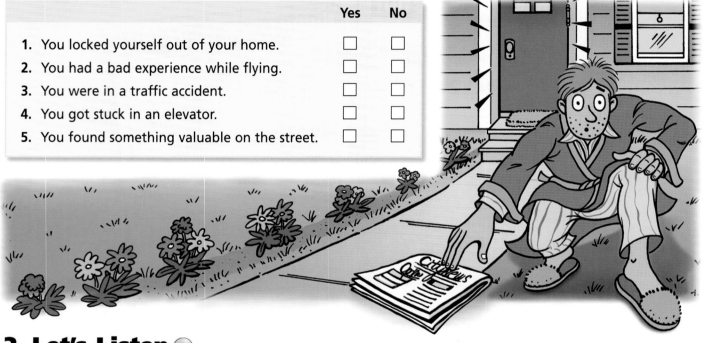

## 2. Let's Listen

Frank is describing what happened to him on Sunday. Listen and number the pictures.

A. ☐

B. ☐

C. ☐ 1

D. ☐

E. ☐

F. ☐

# 3. Let's Listen

Task 1

People are talking about things that happened to them. How do you think each person felt? Listen and check (✓) the correct answer.

|  | Embarrassed | Disappointed | Frightened |
|---|---|---|---|
| 1. | ☐ | ☐ | ☑ |
| 2. | ☐ | ☐ | ☐ |
| 3. | ☐ | ☐ | ☐ |
| 4. | ☐ | ☐ | ☐ |
| 5. | ☐ | ☐ | ☐ |
| 6. | ☐ | ☐ | ☐ |

**Task 2**

Listen again. What do you think each person did next? Circle the correct answer.

1. **a.** opened the door
   **b.** pushed the alarm button
   **c.** used the stairs

2. **a.** bought a plane ticket
   **b.** went back to the terminal
   **c.** opened the briefcase

3. **a.** went back to sleep
   **b.** watched TV
   **c.** left the room quickly

4. **a.** went home
   **b.** went sailing
   **c.** went swimming

5. **a.** turned on the radio
   **b.** slowed down
   **c.** went faster

6. **a.** paid the bill
   **b.** left a big tip
   **c.** called the taxi company

# 4. Let's Listen

Task 1

**People are talking about past events. What happened to them?
Circle the correct answer.**

1.  a. Her car was damaged.
    b. She ran into another car.
    c. Her car got stuck.

2.  a. His plane had mechanical difficulties.
    b. His plane flew into bad weather.
    c. His plane had to make an emergency landing.

3.  a. She got lost in the hotel.
    b. She was stuck in the elevator.
    c. She was locked out of the room.

4.  a. He was injured in the fire.
    b. He escaped from the fire.
    c. He didn't hear the alarm.

5.  a. She won first prize.
    b. Her friend won first prize.
    c. She sold some raffle tickets.

6.  a. He spoke to a famous person.
    b. He saw a famous person.
    c. His wife spoke to a famous person.

Task 2

**Listen again. Are these statements true or false? Check (✓) the correct answer.**

|  | True | False |
| --- | --- | --- |
| 1. Someone in a big truck pulled her out. | ☐ | ☐ |
| 2. The pilot got the airplane out of the storm. | ☐ | ☐ |
| 3. The person from housekeeping didn't have a key. | ☐ | ☐ |
| 4. Only a few people were injured in the fire. | ☐ | ☐ |
| 5. She won a trip to Hawaii. | ☐ | ☐ |
| 6. The rock star signed his menu. | ☐ | ☐ |

# Over to You: Your own story

Task 1

These pictures tell a story. Number them from 1 to 6 and compare your answers
with a partner.

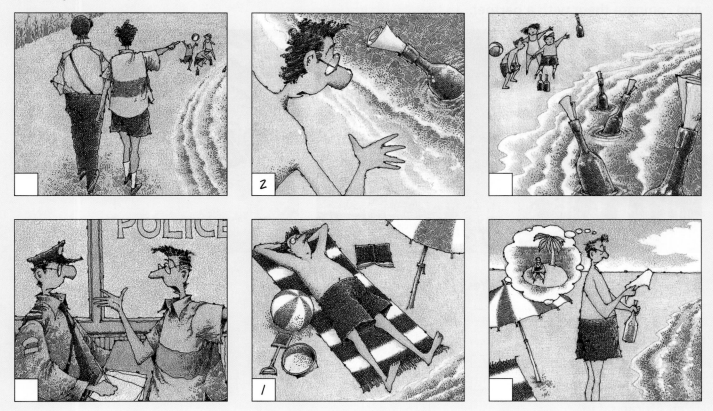

Task 2

Work in pairs. Make up a story based on the pictures. Then tell your story
to another pair.

| Useful expressions | |
| --- | --- |
| First… | message in a bottle |
| Next… | the message said that… |
| Then… | go to the police |
| Meanwhile… | point (v.) |
| Finally… | float (v.) |
| In the end… | wash up on the beach (v.) |

# UNIT 18 Vacations

## 1. Getting Ready

Would you like to take any of these vacations? Check (✓) your answers and compare them with a partner.

|  | Yes | No |
|---|:---:|:---:|
| a bus tour of Europe | ☐ | ☐ |
| a trip to Hawaii | ☐ | ☐ |
| white-water rafting trip | ☐ | ☐ |
| a trip to Disney World | ☐ | ☐ |
| an African safari | ☐ | ☐ |
| other: _____ | ☐ | ☐ |

## 2. Let's Listen

People are discussing vacations with a travel agent. Which trip do they prefer?
Listen and circle the correct answer.

1. **a.** Hawaiian vacation
   **b.** trip to the Philippines

2. **a.** ski vacation
   **b.** Malaysian jungle trip

3. **a.** Nile River trip
   **b.** Australian outback trip

4. **a.** Grand Canyon rafting trip
   **b.** African safari

5. **a.** Southeast Asian trip
   **b.** China tour

6. **a.** European bus trip
   **b.** Russian train trip

# 3. Let's Listen 💿

People are talking about their vacation plans. Will they visit these places?
Listen and check (✓) the correct answers in the charts.

Asia

|  | | Yes | No | How long? |
|---|---|---|---|---|
| 1. | Singapore | ✓ | ☐ | 3 days |
|  | Seoul | ☐ | ☐ | _____ |
|  | Hong Kong | ☐ | ☐ | _____ |
|  | Beijing | ☐ | ☐ | _____ |
|  | Thailand | ☐ | ☐ | _____ |
|  | Tokyo | ☐ | ☐ | _____ |
|  | Malaysia | ☐ | ☐ | _____ |

The UK and Europe

|  | | Yes | No | How long? |
|---|---|---|---|---|
| 2. | London | ☐ | ☐ | _____ |
|  | Oxford | ☐ | ☐ | _____ |
|  | Cambridge | ☐ | ☐ | _____ |
|  | France | ☐ | ☐ | _____ |
|  | Germany | ☐ | ☐ | _____ |
|  | Switzerland | ☐ | ☐ | _____ |
|  | Italy | ☐ | ☐ | _____ |

The United States

|  | | Yes | No | How long? |
|---|---|---|---|---|
| 3. | Los Angeles | ☐ | ☐ | _____ |
|  | San Francisco | ☐ | ☐ | _____ |
|  | Denver | ☐ | ☐ | _____ |
|  | Chicago | ☐ | ☐ | _____ |
|  | Washington, D.C. | ☐ | ☐ | _____ |
|  | New York | ☐ | ☐ | _____ |
|  | Boston | ☐ | ☐ | _____ |

Listen again. How long will they stay in each place? Write the correct
answers in the charts.

# 4. Let's Listen

**Task 1**

People are talking about vacations they want to take. What does each person want to do? Listen and circle the correct answer.

1. **a.** travel alone
   **b.** travel with a friend
   **c.** take a group tour

2. **a.** visit small towns
   **b.** visit big cities
   **c.** stay in expensive hotels

3. **a.** have a boring vacation
   **b.** stay in cheap hotels
   **c.** see and do everything

4. **a.** spend time on a quiet beach
   **b.** spend time in Bangkok
   **c.** see and do everything

5. **a.** spend a month in Mexico City
   **b.** visit a small town
   **c.** travel with other tourists

6. **a.** stay in cheap hotels
   **b.** stay in expensive hotels
   **c.** travel alone

**Task 2**

Listen again. Why do the people want to take the vacations they describe? Write the correct letter.

1. She ___    **a.** has been busy at work.

2. He ___     **b.** wants to practice speaking Spanish.

3. She ___    **c.** heard the beaches are great there.

4. He ___     **d.** wants to be free.

5. She ___    **e.** needs some excitement.

6. He ___     **f.** needs to go somewhere quiet.

# Over to You: Your dream vacation

**Task 1**

Imagine you are taking a trip around the world. What countries would you visit? How long would you stay? What would you do there? Write your answers in the chart.

| | Where would you go? | How long would you stay? | What would you do there? |
|---|---|---|---|
| 1. | _____ | _____ | _____ |
| 2. | _____ | _____ | _____ |
| 3. | _____ | _____ | _____ |
| 4. | _____ | _____ | _____ |
| 5. | _____ | _____ | _____ |

**Task 2**

Work in pairs. Take turns describing your vacations from Task 1. Write your partner's answers in the chart.

| | Where would you go? | How long would you stay? | What would you do there? |
|---|---|---|---|
| 1. | _____ | _____ | _____ |
| 2. | _____ | _____ | _____ |
| 3. | _____ | _____ | _____ |
| 4. | _____ | _____ | _____ |
| 5. | _____ | _____ | _____ |

# UNIT 19 The News

## 1. Getting Ready

Where do you get the news? What kinds of stories interest you?
Check (✓) your answers and compare them with a partner.

**Where do you get the news?**

|  | Often | Sometimes | Rarely |
|---|---|---|---|
| the radio | ☐ | ☐ | ☐ |
| newspapers | ☐ | ☐ | ☐ |
| TV | ☐ | ☐ | ☐ |
| magazines | ☐ | ☐ | ☐ |
| other: _____ | ☐ | ☐ | ☐ |

**What kinds of stories interest you?**

|  | A lot | Somewhat | Not at all |
|---|---|---|---|
| politics | ☐ | ☐ | ☐ |
| sports | ☐ | ☐ | ☐ |
| business | ☐ | ☐ | ☐ |
| entertainment | ☐ | ☐ | ☐ |
| crime | ☐ | ☐ | ☐ |
| other: _____ | ☐ | ☐ | ☐ |

## 2. Let's Listen 🎧

These are the beginnings of news reports. What kind of reports are they?
Listen and circle the correct answer.

1. **a.** politics
   **b.** business

2. **a.** weather
   **b.** traffic

3. **a.** sports
   **b.** crime

4. **a.** sports
   **b.** business

5. **a.** politics
   **b.** entertainment

6. **a.** crime
   **b.** weather

# 3. Let's Listen

**Task 1**

Read these newspaper headlines. Then listen to the news reports.
Are the headlines correct? Check (✓) the answer.

1.

## Guests Escape from Hotel Fire

☐ correct
☐ incorrect

2.

## Restaurant Wins Award for Food

☐ correct
☐ incorrect

3.

## Students Lost for 10 Days Found Safe

☐ correct
☐ incorrect

4.

## Rock Singer's Concert a Great Success

☐ correct
☐ incorrect

5.

## Fishermen Lost During Storm

☐ correct
☐ incorrect

6.

## Panda Babies Born at Zoo

☐ correct
☐ incorrect

**Task 2**

Listen again. Are these statements about things that actually happened or
things that probably happened? Check (✓) the correct answer.

|  | Actually happened | Probably happened |
|---|---|---|
| **1.** The fire started in a guest room. | ☐ | ☑ |
| **2.** More than ten people got food poisoning. | ☐ | ☐ |
| **3.** The students' vehicle broke down. | ☐ | ☐ |
| **4.** Jimmy Wild had a sore throat. | ☐ | ☐ |
| **5.** The boat sank during the storm. | ☐ | ☐ |
| **6.** The baby pandas are very small right now. | ☐ | ☐ |

# 4. Let's Listen

**What are these news reports about? Listen and circle the correct answer.**

1.  **a.** a flood
    **b.** a fire
    **c.** a crime

2.  **a.** a protest
    **b.** an exhibition
    **c.** a sale

3.  **a.** a crime
    **b.** a fire
    **c.** a vacation

4.  **a.** an exhibition
    **b.** a vacation
    **c.** a crime

5.  **a.** a protest
    **b.** an exhibition
    **c.** a sale

6.  **a.** an exhibition
    **b.** a business plan
    **c.** a protest

**Task 2**

**Listen again. Are these statements true or false? Check (✓) the correct answer.**

|  | True | False |
|---|:---:|:---:|
| 1. Many people have had to leave their homes. | ☐ | ☐ |
| 2. Botero's work has been shown in this area before. | ☐ | ☐ |
| 3. The weather is helping the fire spread. | ☐ | ☐ |
| 4. Some of the snakes are still missing. | ☐ | ☐ |
| 5. The farmers support the higher taxes. | ☐ | ☐ |
| 6. The merger could be good news for travelers. | ☐ | ☐ |

# Over to You: What happened?

Task 1

Work in pairs. Choose a picture and write a short news report about it. Use a real situation or your imagination. Answer these questions to get started.

| | |
|---|---|
| What happened? | _____ |
| When? | _____ |
| Where? | _____ |
| Why? | _____ |
| Who was there? | _____ |

Task 2

Find another pair who chose the same picture. Compare your news reports.

# UNIT 20 Opinions

## 1. Getting Ready

Match the topics on the left with the opinions on the right.

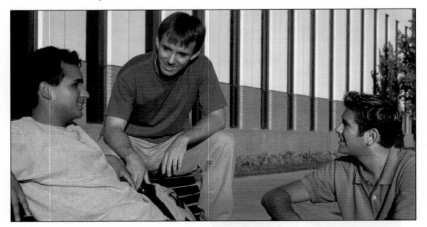

1. smoking _C_

2. religions ___

3. household pets ___

4. the Olympic Games ___

a. They are a great way for people to develop pride in their country.

b. They are dirty, annoying, and should be banned from apartment buildings.

c. It's bad for your health and the health of everyone around you.

d. Their teachings create greater understanding between people.

## 2. Let's Listen

People are expressing opinions. What is the topic of each opinion?
Listen and circle the correct answer.

1. a. the Olympic Games
   b. air travel

2. a. video games
   b. tourism

3. a. TV commercials
   b. rock music

4. a. space exploration
   b. medical research

5. a. winter sports
   b. bungee jumping

6. a. lotteries
   b. pets

# 3. Let's Listen 🎧

**Task 1**

People are giving opinions about these topics. Are they for or against them?
Listen and check (✓) the correct answer.

|  | For | Against |
|---|---|---|
| **1.** space exploration | ☐ | ☐ |
| **2.** TV commercials | ☐ | ☐ |
| **3.** the Olympic Games | ☐ | ☐ |
| **4.** lotteries | ☐ | ☐ |
| **5.** action movies | ☐ | ☐ |
| **6.** pets | ☐ | ☐ |

**Task 2**

Listen again. What reason does each person give? Circle the correct answer.

1. **a.** It's too expensive.
   **b.** It's how we learn about the universe.
   **c.** It isn't important.

2. **a.** They're too short.
   **b.** They interrupt his favorite programs.
   **c.** They're boring.

3. **a.** They encourage an interest in sports.
   **b.** They cost too much.
   **c.** Her country never wins.

4. **a.** They're dangerous.
   **b.** They're fun to play.
   **c.** They raise money for the city.

5. **a.** They're too violent.
   **b.** They're too boring.
   **c.** They're too loud.

6. **a.** They don't have anywhere to play.
   **b.** They don't eat enough food.
   **c.** They cost too much.

# 4. Let's Listen

Task 1

People are giving their opinions. Do they agree? Listen and check (✓) the correct answer.

| | Agree | Don't agree |
|---|---|---|
| 1. | ☑ | ☐ |
| 2. | ☐ | ☐ |
| 3. | ☐ | ☐ |
| 4. | ☐ | ☐ |
| 5. | ☐ | ☐ |
| 6. | ☐ | ☐ |

Task 2

Listen again. Are these statements true or false? Check (✓) the correct answer.

| | | True | False |
|---|---|---|---|
| 1. | He thinks Spanish is hard to learn. | ☐ | ☐ |
| 2. | She thinks lawyers work hard. | ☐ | ☐ |
| 3. | He thinks most TV programs are for old people. | ☐ | ☐ |
| 4. | He had to wait an hour for the bus. | ☐ | ☐ |
| 5. | She likes to try things on before she buys them. | ☐ | ☐ |
| 6. | The rain is good for her garden. | ☐ | ☐ |

# Over to You: That's true, but...

Choose three topics from the box and write them in the chart.
Write your opinion about each topic.

| the Olympic Games | foreign language education |
|---|---|
| pets | television programs |
| space exploration | commercials |
| lotteries | public transportation |
| action movies | the Internet |

| | Topic | Opinion |
|---|---|---|
| 1. | the Olympic Games | They are a great way to develop pride in your country. |
| 2. | _____ | _____ |
| 3. | _____ | _____ |
| 4. | _____ | _____ |

Task 2

Work in groups. Share your opinions with your group. Give reasons.
Do you agree or disagree with your group members' opinions?

**Example:** **A:** I think the Olympic Games are a good idea.
They're a great way to develop pride in
your country.

**B:** That's true, but I think the Olympic Games are
too expensive. Countries should use that money
to help the poor.

### Useful expressions

You're right.

I totally agree.

I agree with some of that.

I know what you're saying, but…

That's true, but…

Really? I think…

# UNIT 21 Famous People

## 1. Getting Ready

Match the famous people on the left with the descriptions on the right.

1. Leonardo Da Vinci _e_        a. She changed her name to Marilyn Monroe.

2. Mozart ___                   b. He was an actor who became a U.S. president.

3. Norma Jean Baker ___         c. He invented the lightbulb.

4. Ronald Reagan ___            d. He wrote his first piece of music at the age of five.

5. Thomas Edison ___            e. He painted the *Mona Lisa*.

6. Jacqueline Onassis ___       f. She was married to a U.S. president.

## 2. Let's Listen

These conversations are about famous people. Listen and circle each famous person's job.

1. a. political leader       3. a. actor       5. a. actor
   b. actress                   b. writer          b. singer

2. a. political leader       4. a. painter     6. a. singer
   b. actor                     b. athlete         b. scientist

# 3. Let's Listen

Task 1

People are discussing the life of the actor James Dean. Did these events in Dean's life happen in Indiana, California, or New York? Listen and check (✓) the correct answer.

|  | Indiana | California | New York |
|---|---|---|---|
| 1. He was born. | ✓ | ☐ | ☐ |
| 2. His mother passed away. | ☐ | ☐ | ☐ |
| 3. He lived with his aunt and uncle. | ☐ | ☐ | ☐ |
| 4. He went to college. | ☐ | ☐ | ☐ |
| 5. He did more stage acting. | ☐ | ☐ | ☐ |
| 6. He died in a car crash. | ☐ | ☐ | ☐ |

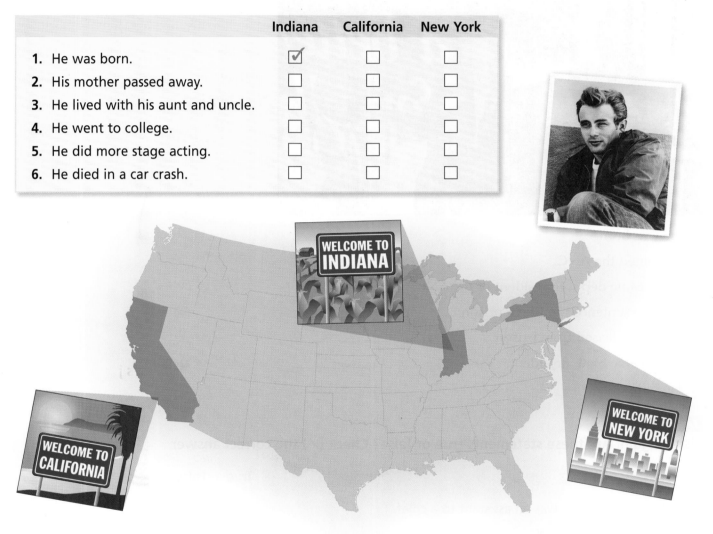

Task 2

Listen again. How did James Dean become famous? Number the events from 1 to 6.

He won an award as "Most Promising Newcomer." ___

He had a starring role in *East of Eden*. ___

He acted in school plays. _1_

He went to college. ___

*Rebel Without a Cause* made him famous. ___

He did modeling for advertisements. ___

# 4. Let's Listen

This person is talking about the life of the South African leader Nelson Mandela.
When did these events happen? Listen and write the years.

1. He was born. _____1918_____

2. He joined the ANC. _____

3. He became deputy president of the ANC. _____

4. He was sentenced to life in prison. _____

5. He was released from prison. _____

6. He became State President. _____

7. He retired. _____

Task 2

Listen again. Are these statements true or false? Check (✓) the correct answer.

|  | True | False |
|---|---|---|
| 1. Mandela's father was an assistant to a chief. | ☐ | ☐ |
| 2. Mandela studied law. | ☐ | ☐ |
| 3. The ANC encouraged people to be violent. | ☐ | ☐ |
| 4. Mandela helped poor people stay on the land where they lived. | ☐ | ☐ |
| 5. Even while he was in prison, he inspired people. | ☐ | ☐ |
| 6. As soon as he was released from prison, he retired. | ☐ | ☐ |

# Over to You: Before they were famous

Task 1
Work in groups. Choose a famous person everyone in your group knows.
Then complete the form.

| | |
|---|---|
| Name | _____ |
| Occupation | _____ |
| Born/Died | _____ |
| Education | _____ |
| Childhood | _____ |
| | _____ |
| Achievements | _____ |
| | _____ |
| Other | _____ |
| | _____ |

Task 2
Work in new groups. Tell your group members about the famous person you chose.

# UNIT 22 Food and Nutrition

## 1. Getting Ready

**Find these foods in the nutrition pyramid. Write the correct letter next to each item.**

1. ice cream _B_
2. apples ___
3. noodles ___
4. chicken ___
5. hamburgers ___
6. candy ___
7. carrots ___
8. pancakes ___
9. pineapples ___
10. tuna ___

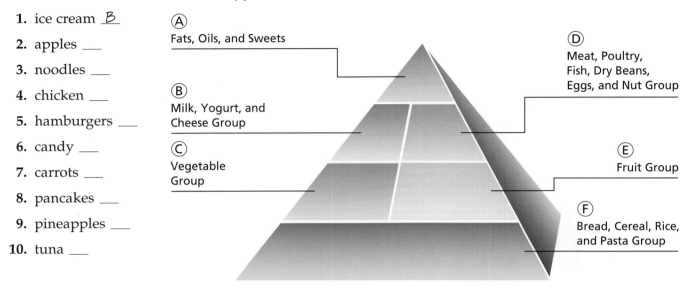

Ⓐ Fats, Oils, and Sweets

Ⓑ Milk, Yogurt, and Cheese Group

Ⓒ Vegetable Group

Ⓓ Meat, Poultry, Fish, Dry Beans, Eggs, and Nut Group

Ⓔ Fruit Group

Ⓕ Bread, Cereal, Rice, and Pasta Group

## 2. Let's Listen 💿

**People are talking about their eating habits. What does each person eat now?**
**Listen and check (✓) the correct picture.**

1.
  a.
  b.

2.
  a.
  b.

3.
  a.
  b.

4.
  a.
  b.

# 3. Let's Listen

Task 1

A doctor is talking to her patients about nutrition. What advice does she give each person? Listen and circle the correct answer.

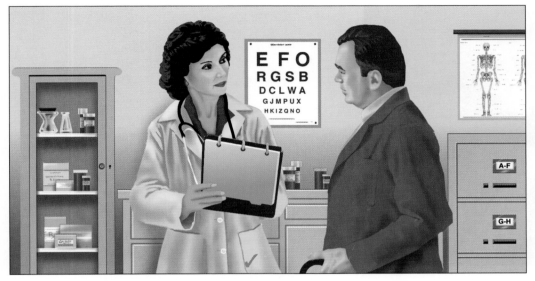

1. a. eat fewer vegetables
   b. eat less cheese
   c. eat a lot of fat

2. a. don't eat fish
   b. eat more vegetables
   c. eat more fruit

3. a. eat less meat
   b. eat less fruit
   c. eat more meat

4. a. eat less bread
   b. eat more meat
   c. eat less fruit

5. a. eat more eggs and cheese
   b. don't eat cheese
   c. eat more vegetables

6. a. eat less meat
   b. don't eat chocolate
   c. eat more vegetables

Task 2

Listen again. What is each person's health problem? Write the correct letter.

1. Mr. Grant _d_          a. is losing too much weight.

2. Linda ___              b. has a skin problem.

3. Chris ___              c. needs to lose weight.

4. Ms. Barton ___         d. has high cholesterol.

5. Mr. O'Brien ___        e. has been feeling tired and weak.

6. Mrs. Johnson ___       f. has high blood pressure.

# 4. Let's Listen 💿

This person is giving a talk about cheese. Are these statements true or false?
Listen and check (✓) the correct answer.

|  | True | False |
|---|:---:|:---:|
| 1. Cheese was first made over 3,000 years ago. | ✓ | ☐ |
| 2. Cheese contains vitamins. | ☐ | ☐ |
| 3. Most cheese in the United States is made from goat's milk. | ☐ | ☐ |
| 4. Cheese doesn't contain water. | ☐ | ☐ |
| 5. The process of making cheese was probably discovered by chance. | ☐ | ☐ |
| 6. Pasteurized milk contains bacteria. | ☐ | ☐ |
| 7. The bacteria cultures never release carbon dioxide. | ☐ | ☐ |
| 8. Curd is a liquid. | ☐ | ☐ |

Task 2

Listen again. How is cheese made? Number the steps from 1 to 5.

The milk forms a solid substance. ___

Specially cultivated bacteria are added to the milk. ___

The milk is heated to remove all bacteria. _1_

The curd is removed and drained. ___

The milk is kept warm so the cultures can grow. ___

# Over to You: Is your diet healthy?

Task 1

**What have you eaten in the last three days? Write your answers in the chart and compare them with a partner.**

|  | You | Your partner |
|---|---|---|
| Last three breakfasts: | | |
| | | |
| | | |
| Last three lunches: | | |
| | | |
| | | |
| Last three dinners: | | |
| | | |
| | | |
| Last three snacks: | | |
| | | |
| | | |

Task 2

**Work in pairs. Has your partner been eating nutritiously? Suggest foods your partner should eat more or less often.**

**Example:** I see you've had five cans of soda in the last three days.
That's too much sugar. Instead, I think you should…

Fats, Oils, and Sweets

Milk, Yogurt, and Cheese Group

Vegetable Group

Meat, Poultry, Fish, Dry Beans, Eggs, and Nut Group

Fruit Group

Bread, Cereal, Rice, and Pasta Group

# UNIT 23 Predicaments

## 1. Getting Ready

What would you do if you were in these predicaments? Write your answers in the chart and compare them with a partner.

| Predicament | Solution |
|---|---|
| 1. Your neighbors make a lot of noise at night. | _____ |
| 2. You forgot a friend's birthday. | _____ |
| 3. A friend owes you money. | _____ |
| 4. A classmate asks you for a loan. | _____ |
| 5. A classmate cheats on tests. | _____ |

## 2. Let's Listen

Listen to the conversations. What is each person's predicament?
Circle the correct answer.

1. a. He doesn't want his guest to leave.
   b. He doesn't know when his guest will leave.

2. a. Her friend forgot to pay some money back.
   b. She forgot to pay back some money to a friend.

3 a. She wants to invite her co-worker out.
   b. A co-worker is always inviting her out.

4. a. His friend never lends things.
   b. His friend never returns things.

5. a. He forgot about his friend's party.
   b. His forgot to bring a gift to the party.

6. a. The neighbor's dog barks a lot.
   b. The neighbor's dog is always outside.

# 3. Let's Listen

## Task 1

People are telling stories about predicaments that happened to them.
Listen and number the pictures.

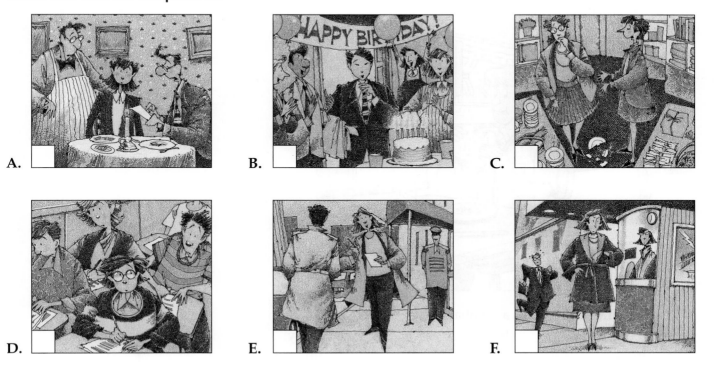

A.

B.

C.

D.

E.

F.

## Task 2

Listen again. How does each story end? Circle the correct answer.

1. a. She ran away.
   b. She had to pay for the plate.
   c. She didn't have to pay for the plate.

2. a. He had to pay for everything.
   b. He had to pay for the things he ordered.
   c. He didn't have to pay for anything.

3. a. His girlfriend was very upset.
   b. His girlfriend wasn't upset.
   c. His girlfriend left before he arrived.

4. a. He said that he wasn't Tom Cruise.
   b. He signed Tom Cruise's name.
   c. He signed his own name.

5. a. They had the party in a restaurant.
   b. They cleaned the apartment.
   c. They didn't have the party.

6. a. He asked to sit somewhere else.
   b. He told the teacher the guy was cheating.
   c. He wrote the wrong answers on his test.

# 4. Let's Listen

### Task 1

People are talking about predicaments. How does each person feel?
Listen and circle the correct answer.

1. a. embarrassed
   b. angry
   c. amused

2. a. depressed
   b. angry
   c. embarrassed

3. a. embarrassed
   b. angry
   c. confused

4. a. angry
   b. unconcerned
   c. depressed

5. a. worried
   b. angry
   c. amused

6. a. angry
   b. worried
   c. embarrassed

### Task 2

Listen again. What is each person planning to do about the situation?
Write the correct letter.

1. ___        a. nothing

2. ___        b. call the manager

3. ___        c. talk to his parents

4. ___        d. speak to his wife

5. ___        e. sleep in a different room

6. ___        f. send him a note

# Over to You: What would you do?

Task 1

Work in pairs. Read each predicament. Then write a solution for each one.

1. Your best friend just got a driver's license and gave you a ride home. You saw your friend accidentally run over your little brother's bike when he was leaving. Your parents are angry and want to know what happened.

   Solution: _____

   _____

   _____

2. You accepted a date for Saturday night with someone you think is okay. Then the person you really like calls you and asks for a date for the same Saturday night.

   Solution: _____

   _____

   _____

3. There's a concert coming up that you're excited to see. It's impossible to get tickets. Someone you don't like very much invites you to go.

   Solution: _____

   _____

   _____

Task 2

Work in groups. Read your solutions aloud. Discuss the solutions you hear for each predicament and vote for the best one.

# UNIT 24 Global Issues

## 1. Getting Ready

**How important are these issues to you? Check (✓) your answers and compare them with a partner.**

| | Very important | Somewhat important | Not important |
|---|:---:|:---:|:---:|
| air pollution | ☐ | ☐ | ☐ |
| water pollution | ☐ | ☐ | ☐ |
| destruction of the rain forests | ☐ | ☐ | ☐ |
| terrorism | ☐ | ☐ | ☐ |
| crime | ☐ | ☐ | ☐ |
| global warming | ☐ | ☐ | ☐ |
| overpopulation | ☐ | ☐ | ☐ |
| AIDS | ☐ | ☐ | ☐ |
| poverty | ☐ | ☐ | ☐ |
| war | ☐ | ☐ | ☐ |
| unemployment | ☐ | ☐ | ☐ |
| other: _____ | ☐ | ☐ | ☐ |

## 2. Let's Listen 💿

**People are talking about issues. Which issue do they think is most important right now? Listen and circle the correct answer.**

1. **a.** water pollution
   **b.** air pollution

2. **a.** unemployment
   **b.** crime

3. **a.** public transportation
   **b.** housing

4. **a.** education
   **b.** unemployment

5. **a.** public transportation
   **b.** unemployment

6. **a.** overpopulation
   **b.** AIDS

# 3. Let's Listen 💿

**Task 1**

What issues are these people talking about? Listen and circle the correct answer.

1. **a.** air pollution
   **b.** water pollution
   **c.** overpopulation

2. **a.** global warming
   **b.** water pollution
   **c.** unemployment

3. **a.** poverty
   **b.** overpopulation
   **c.** war

4. **a.** crime
   **b.** traffic
   **c.** air pollution

5. **a.** air pollution
   **b.** garbage
   **c.** unemployment

6. **a.** housing
   **b.** poverty
   **c.** crime

**Task 2**

Listen again. Are these statements true or false? Check (✓) the correct answer.

|  | True | False |
|---|---|---|
| 1. He wants to be the mayor of his city. | ☐ | ☐ |
| 2. She's going to move to Chicago. | ☐ | ☐ |
| 3. He reads a lot of sports magazines. | ☐ | ☐ |
| 4. She bought a new car. | ☐ | ☐ |
| 5. She started recycling her garbage. | ☐ | ☐ |
| 6. He moved to a small apartment downtown. | ☐ | ☐ |

# 4. Let's Listen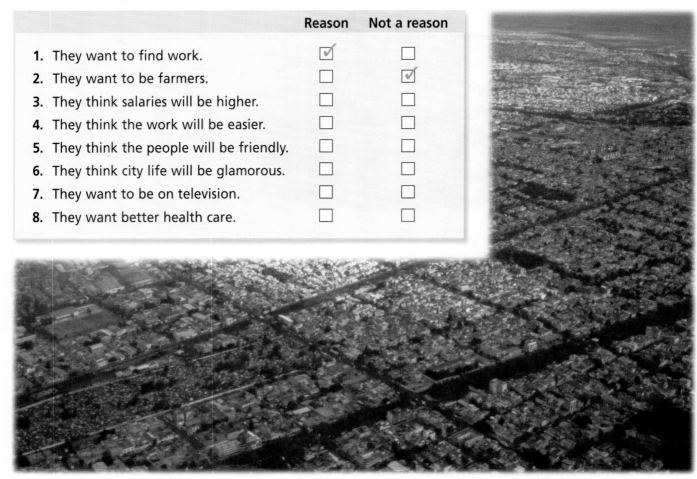

Listen to a talk on very large cities, or "megacities." Why do people move from the country to a megacity? Listen and check (✓) the reasons you hear.

|  | Reason | Not a reason |
|---|---|---|
| 1. They want to find work. | ✓ | ☐ |
| 2. They want to be farmers. | ☐ | ✓ |
| 3. They think salaries will be higher. | ☐ | ☐ |
| 4. They think the work will be easier. | ☐ | ☐ |
| 5. They think the people will be friendly. | ☐ | ☐ |
| 6. They think city life will be glamorous. | ☐ | ☐ |
| 7. They want to be on television. | ☐ | ☐ |
| 8. They want better health care. | ☐ | ☐ |

**Task 2**

Listen again. Are these statements true or false? Check (✓) the correct answer.

|  | True | False |
|---|---|---|
| 1. Jobs are often difficult to find in megacities. | ☐ | ☐ |
| 2. Salaries in megacities are very low. | ☐ | ☐ |
| 3. Many people end up in huge, expensive houses. | ☐ | ☐ |
| 4. Health care is much cheaper in megacities. | ☐ | ☐ |
| 5. Air pollution is a problem in megacities. | ☐ | ☐ |
| 6. The problems in megacities are becoming easier. | ☐ | ☐ |

# Over to You: The most serious problems

**Work in groups. What are the three most serious problems in your city or country? What should be done about them? Write your ideas in the chart.**

Example:  **A:** What do you think are the most serious problems in…?

**B:** I think…is the biggest problem. They should… Don't you think so?

**C:** Yes, I think so, too. / No, personally, I think…

**D:** I'd have to agree with you. / Really? I think….

| Problems | Solutions |
|---|---|
| 1. _____ | _____ |
| | _____ |
| | _____ |
| 2. _____ | _____ |
| | _____ |
| | _____ |
| 3. _____ | _____ |
| | _____ |
| | _____ |